C0-ATB-330

WORSHIP WAYS FOR CAMP

WORSHIP WAYS FOR CAMP

CLARICE M. BOWMAN

ASSOCIATION PRESS
NEW YORK

Association Press, 291 Broadway, New York 7, N. Y.

Library of Congress catalog card number: 55-7408

 55

Printed in the United States of America
American Book–Stratford Press, Inc., New York

To my little niece

CATHERINE

Foreword

CAMPERS always busy themselves learning languages. There is the language of the woodland—the bark, the leaves, the roots, special life-ways of each tree and of the brotherhood of trees. There is the language of the water, whether it be jolly brook or lively mountain river, sky-mirroring lake or majestic ocean waves. There is the language of the weather. There is star language. And there are the messages of the good earth.

Then there is a world of fun in increasing one's knowledge of how to communicate in the languages of people. In addition to the spoken word, there are ways of sending messages by the use of flags, by smoke signals, the Indian signs; there are fascinating codes to be deciphered, and new ones to be devised. For whenever human beings get together, they try to tell one another what they see and hear and touch and, more importantly, what they feel inside. There is, too, the silent language that is so effective when campers are gathered around a closing campfire. No one breathes a word, yet all understand and feel close—close to one another and, somehow, to Another.

It is this language of worship ways this book talks about. But for meanings to be known, deep inside, we must live the thoughts and pray the prayers and love our brothers and God. The same God of early Bible times, of all Christendom's history, seems to be *here,* in our camp. We ourselves find, as we speak from our hearts, some worship ways to tell God and one another our thoughts. We sometimes feel that Someone we know loves us very much really talks to us. He helps us want to be our utmost best—not just for our own sake, not just for the sake of those we love, but for His sake. When we have hard things to face, He is our Friend.

Churches and synagogues and groups of many different kinds have, through the centuries, worked out their special languages of worship ways. Camps do, too. The hope that prompts our sending out this little book, with a few printed pages carrying others' thoughts about worshiping God, is that in *your* camp it will be a silent yet ready friend, not intruding, but helping when needed. May something here be as a spark from the campfire, lifting thoughts to God.

Those who have shared in bringing this book into being are a vast campfire circle. Some lived and wrote long ago; many are living now. Many are boys and girls who in camp took a bit of time to write down their thoughts about God and the way He would have us live. Many are adult campers who did the same. And in our campfire circle are some of long, long ago, before even our Bibles were written down; like us today, they looked up into God's sky and felt His love speak in their hearts. To all these, our utmost thanks; and to all who have given permission as authors or publishers to use their material, our continuing gratitude. Now—we clasp hands, left hand over, with the new campers to come!

CLARICE M. BOWMAN

Contents

PART III: WITH JUNIORS AND YOUNG TEENS

PART ONE

THE WAY OF WORSHIP

1

Thinking Together about Worship

WHAT DO *you* say that worship is?

No one of us can speak for the experiences of another. To each alone is the inner "witness," the awareness of having felt need for a relationship beyond the human, the realization at times, somehow, of Response.

For us to think together about worship—you, the reader, and I, the author—it is not needful that we speak in the same words or phrases, or even that we think in the same thought forms. Our backgrounds of earlier training and present customs may differ. We may be of different churches or brotherhoods or even faiths. To some, the word "worship" may bring a picture of a reverent congregation in a dim, vaulted sanctuary joining hearts and voices earnestly in the decorous rhythms of a highly ritualistic service. To others, the word may signify ecstatic "Amens" of spiritually exuberant country folk in their white-frame meetinghouse. Others may think first of informal, spontaneous moments in children's groups, and of a look of wonder on young faces. Others may see in their mind's eye a camp group of young teens meditating in silence on a hillside.

But through all our experiences, if they are in truth

"worship," there is a focal centering toward the One God, the God of all the universe and of all our lives. To prepare for worship means to reach consciously toward the divine with thought, feeling, will.

We interpret our experiences in many ways, like a prism bending light into a rainbow of colors. We build up over the years our customs and forms. We make music. We say prayers. We meditate. We dedicate. But through the centuries, and from the testimony of millions, there seems to run a strange agreement, first as to people's need for achieving some kind of relationship with God, and second as to an inner sensing that there has been communication. One prays, and life is different. One reaches up one's hand however timidly through the dark, and it is taken hold of.

Who takes one step toward God through doubtings dim,
God comes a thousand miles in blazing light to him.[1]

But the "difference," when one has truly worshiped, does not stop with a momentary flash of feeling. The man who has felt the touch of God's love upon his innermost soul goes forth to see his neighbors, however unloving they may be toward him, from more of a "God's-eye" point of view. The forgiveness vouchsafed him so undeserving he must pass on to others. Chords of sympathy once more vibrate in his heart; and he must do something about the evils that hold back his brothers from fullness of life.

Had mankind never worshiped, had man's thoughts never lifted higher than his own self-involvement, is there not question as to whether any progress in human relationships would have been made? Furies of passion and greed and lust might have consumed the human race long since. But man does lift his face from the clod. He feels shining on it the light of God. And in that light, he sees himself anew—his very body as a miracle of creation, his days as fraught with purpose. He looks at his fellows as beings akin, each needing rightfully that which he would most wish for himself and his own. And from time to time he dreams of a better way for all, and puts his shoulder to the plow for the achieving of it.

Thus in humanity's long trek upward, there have been bending-points of history: times when one or more individuals dared to stand forth and thunder against practices that harmed or hurt. And there is still the haunting awareness that all is not yet well. A God of illimitable love for all still calls to us.

When individuals worship, something happens. They experience new life. One blinded by self-concern feels the mists dispel, and he sees God and others and self in truer light. One crippled and warped in mind or body feels new exhilaration. One pulled in many directions by conflicting desires feels himself made whole again. And these go out to spread a new radiance, a joy. There is an infusion of life abundant into the sick bloodstream of the world. Chain-reacting love melts hate. The light of increased understanding replaces the darkness of ignorance, superstition, mistrust. Love triumphs over hate, light over dark, life over death. This is the nuclear miracle.

Step by Step in Worship and Prayer

The first step in real worship is the Godward reach, the willingness to "let go, let God." An individual meditating alone during his daily prayer time takes this step as he excludes other thoughts; he focuses mind, heart, and will upon the love of God. In this readiness of spirit he affirms his belief that there is a God. He tries to still his inward turmoils, that he may be led to God. A congregation must needs do likewise. Each individual is a responsible conductor (or nonconductor) of the spiritual current. In a worshiping camp, the beginning of worship is not the moment a leader announces an opening hymn, but rather, this upward reaching on the part of each one. Whether a camper is completely sure of his beliefs or not he can be inwardly quiet and expectant.

True worship is always from the inside out. It is felt in the soul. And whatever is done outwardly, such as singing or praying, is but expression sincerely and naturally of what was first felt. Each is responsible before God for himself. That is why no priest or leader can perform our worship for us. That is why going through motions in a ready-made "program" or merely reading materials, no matter how fitting, is not enough. The true worship prayer is: "Breathe on me, breath of God." Then His "life anew" will fill us and make us clean and help us "do what Thou wouldst do."

Prayer and worship are intensely active experiences. There is no place for silly sentimentalism or escapism. The soul and its God grapple together, veritably, like Jacob wrestling with the angel. As weak humans, we dislike being known. We fear the light. We love our pet sins. We hold on to self-love. But the individual feels a power beyond his own working within him—even in his stubborn thoughts. He is cleansed, made whole. He feels new depths of love and sympathy and compassion for other people.

2

Camping and the Worship Adventure

ALREADY A FULL-FLEDGED MOVEMENT, camping is one of the most healthful influences of the century, physically, mentally, socially, spiritually.

Camping takes individuals, whatever their ages and just as they are, into wholesome environments. It brings them close to sources—the earth, the air, the sea, the sky. It surrounds them with human fellowship. Humor, good will, and joy are in the very atmosphere. Camp tears away subterfuges and camouflages, and bids the growing personality stand strong and firm, with a cleaner, saner set of values.

Camping deals with the whole of life. It helps make life whole. Even in short-term camps we see it happen. Youngsters come as tense bundles of swirling inner conflicts; they learn (often not without pain and struggle) to "pull themselves together"; they go forth happier, more vibrant, more nearly whole selves. Some have known only disruption in their earlier lives—broken homes, constant moving, quarrels. Camp provides an overarching wholeness of group fellowship. They return to their homes knowing a little better how to get along with others. Their feet are set on the road toward being society's problem-solvers, not its problems.

All these are *spiritual* values. But they do not "just happen"! Camp leaders in private, agency, and other camps are realizing that the right kind of preparation is needful.

The approach to worship that we affirm is vigorous, honest. In camp we try to be vigorous, honest, in all that we do. We "give the fullest spirit play." We know the joyous abandon of play and laughter, the wind whipping about us as we climb hard, the warm companionship with one another at evenfall. Real worship belongs in camp, not as an extra, but naturally. There is no time of the day or night, no activity, in which worship would not be fitting. Worship may "happen" at any time. But there must be some preparation.

All the Leaders

Preparing so that worship may be real in camp is not merely a matter of selecting a worship counselor or chaplain. It is rather a matter of the spirit in all who walk with campers moment by moment.

Can they *wonder?* Have those chosen to be leaders in the camp life an eager, questing, childlike quality of spirit? Can they stand enthralled by the mysteries of moonlight, or breathe more quickly at the sudden flash of a redbird's wing? Can they discover—and uncover for eager campers—universes in the rainbow-hued droplet of water on the grass in the early morn? Are they *learners,* ever widening their eyes and hearts to take in new horizons of truth, and seeing it all as God's truth?

Can they feel *with* campers? This is more than asking whether they understand the particular age level with which they are assigned. True, they will have studied and come to love growing persons of this age level. But more than that. Are they quiet-hearted, listening individuals who, when there is a moment of wonder, will not pry ruthlessly, or say the wrong thing, or say too much? Can they give just the needed spark of enthusiasm that will touch off still more in the camper, helping him to think, to feel, to say *for himself?*

Are they patient, quiet and uncluttered inside, able to forget the clock at times and to forego their own ego-need to tell what they know, so that they will wait until campers themselves discover and relate their thoughts in their very own ways?

Some Times of Readiness for High Moments

In a good camp, the days are not too hurried. The tempo is natural, steady. There is time enough. The campers' own plans (and the campers, even the little tykes, are the ones who should make the plans) are guided tactfully. Campers must be helped not to attempt too much for the time available or for their own energies and zest.

Several kinds of experiences may prepare them for a moment of "thinking with God" that might even be called "worship" or "prayer":

Discovery times, when something new comes upon the scene, or is found at a bend of the trail. And one catches one's breath with: "Thank You, God, for thinking this and making it, and for giving us eyes to see and minds to know, and especially thank You for the fun we're having together."

Problem times, when something is bothering somebody in the group, or perhaps something is bothering the whole crowd. After talking it through, or even before, campers may want to pray: "Help us, God. Keep our thoughts clear, don't let them get muddled up with anger. May we choose wisely. Help us be good sports in following through."

Fun times: "Thanks so much, O God, for all this merry laughter, and the glad songs, and the silly games, and the jolly jokes. Thanks for the food! Help us to help others be happy all our lives."

Thinking times, when some new information is being shared, an exhibit interpreted, a drama given, ideas discussed: "Here we are, O God, trying our very best to get all these wonderful new ideas straight. You who planned it all know that we want to understand things aright. Keep us patient, so that we will keep on trying to find out, and not stop short of the real answers. Thank You for our minds. We like the fun of thinking for ourselves. You knew, when You made us, didn't You, that we would want to think and choose for ourselves? Sometimes we feel that You are thinking right along with us. We need You to lead us. Amen."

Times of concern, when someone may be hurt or worried, or when campers remember hungry or lonely people anywhere: "God, we people of Yours aren't doing a very good job of looking after one another. We raise food, and then fail to get it distributed where the hungry people are. We have warm clothing, but we let people go cold without enough to keep them warm. We have shelters, but many wander homeless. We have friendly feelings in our hearts, but many are lonely, as if they didn't have a friend in all the world. We keep too much of all the good things to ourselves. We indulge and pamper ourselves like a bunch of softies. We shut our minds tight and do not think of others' needs. Touch us now, even though it hurts us very much to think of these things. And make us more loving and kindly in our hearts. Help us stop and think when we start to buy extra candies or soft drinks for ourselves. Show us what ways we may go about helping others, beginning right now. And may we grow up to be good influences, in helping You bring about a friendlier world."

Thus, in the buoyant camping day, the high and luminous moments come. Campers will grow in spiritual stature. Maybe some will grow up to be, not only physically vigorous and stalwart, but pilot lives whose example others may safely follow.

How Can We Plan for High Moments?

We do not, as counselors, begin our preparations by setting down neat plans on paper, or in any way attempting to prepackage the high moments. We begin by preparing ourselves, mind and heart and soul as well as physically fit body. *And God does the rest!* We may sensitize our minds by devotional habits, and our hearts by love of the campers. We may have songs and ideas and Scripture "on the tip of our hearts" so that when the right moment comes, we or the campers may be led to say *just enough.* (But woe to us if we are walking "famous-quotation" spouters!)

Nor can we schedule "spontaneous" worship. In fact, we wonder how anyone (even a minister) can guarantee that what will happen at a certain hour will be *worship.* For the Divine has a part to play. And the mood of the group itself will determine readiness or unreadiness. An advance bulletin promoting a big youth conference promised, "Stupendous worship experience!" We cannot help feeling that in something like inverse ratio to our own arrogance will vital, stirring worship come.

Rather than attempting to schedule such moments of worship, we are guided by campers' thoughts and needs —we do it "by ear," not by the clock. After all, we well know that fun takes place at many times in addition to the special times scheduled for fun. Learning does, too. So will worship.

However, there are certain outstanding "seasons" of camp life and ways of meeting their special challenge.

At the Beginning

Camp begins, of course, the minute the first camper arrives; that is, it begins in terms of the current group fellowship. Actually, the beginning goes back to the dream, the goals, the choosing of counselors and staff, the training, the anticipation.

The camper piles out of the family car. Finding his quarters and getting acquainted with his new "family" group is his first big venture. The counselors' ease in meeting him, their genuine welcome and helpfulness, will establish an island of security in the midst of a sea of newness.

The first all-camp gathering is electric with expectancy. Surely an expression of thankfulness to the God who made it all possible would be in order. Whatever the particular symbolism or form of expression used, a bowing of the head before a Power above gives a new dimension to camp life. Camp is more than the geographical boundaries of the camp site.

Some camps raise the nation's flag as their ceremonial for launching camp. In one, campers found the little wild flag or iris and used it in a central setting, with meditation about the Creator who made the whole earth, and his little blue "flag" that grows in many parts. Some camps raise the Christian flag. In one camp, the country's flag stood on one side of the leaders' stand, while an evergreen tree of similar height placed on the other side symbolized the Maker of all good things and His ever-present guidance.

Putting camp activities into operation involves planning. All the campers—the little ones, as truly as the bigger ones—should have part in planning what concerns them. Surely, in the serious little discussion groups, it would not be out of place to talk with God a bit about keeping the plans wise and kind, and productive of the very best possibilities for all.

Sometimes the health and safety observances seem to be stern duties, and an aura of force surrounds them. But this is unwise psychologically, as well as untrue democratically. Campers need to be helped to see why such observances should be upheld under all circumstances, whether or not one is under the watchful eye of a counselor. There might be, too, a spirit of thankfulness for the gift of health, and for foresight to avoid dangers and help others do so.

In the Living Group

In most camps a small group will live together, hiking, exploring, building all sorts of things together. Soon after the camper arrives, he begins to get acquainted with his buddies. On the first evening, when it comes time for "day's end," there may be woven into the conversation an expression of thankfulness to God for bringing together all these persons from different places. The counselor will be at ease and friendly. If there is to be a spoken prayer he may give it, rather than plunge any camper into immediate embarrassment. His attitude should be that God is a part of the family group.

Not only on the first night, but on all evenings, this talk-over time is a very special hour. All the lights may be out, or there may be one candle burning. By and by campers will look forward to these moments when they may talk over anything they want to, good or bad, glad or sad. From time to time the counselor or the campers will plan pleasant surprises for this hour. Day's end is a quiet, relaxed period, generating warm securities that encourage sound sleep and ensure a bouncing time on the morrow.

Never should a counselor be so crude and insensitive as to force stilted, prepared programs on the group at this hour. This is a group talk-it-over time. The counselor's best part is to help campers feel utterly free to say what *they* wish. To be sure, he too may have made some delightful discovery he would like to tell them about. In fact, all campers soon acquire the habit of "saving up" something special to share at this time. Conversations do not need to be prolonged. Some evenings the campers may be tired, ready to turn in. At other times, there may be need for a quiet talk-fest, if there is a real problem (and not just filibustering to postpone going to bed). In his living group, every camper should feel free to be his real self. He can feel *accepted.*

Certainly any disturbances of the fellowship feeling in the group itself need to be ironed out. "Only as we forgive" can we truly pray or prepare for sleep.

Would any materials be used in this cabin time? Perhaps. Some seed thoughts for day's end may be found in this book. A bit of a story might sometime be in order, a poem, a few lines of Scripture, undoubtedly a song.

But let the campers' own conversation set the pace. Some of the bigger boys and girls might select a thought and share it. Better, they might write their own thoughts!

The writer is aware that in some camp groups there is reluctance on the part of administration and counselors to open the way for such free discussion and prayer. In those circumstances, a suitable thought might be prepared for the evening, choosing carefully one that will be acceptable to campers of whatever faiths or backgrounds are represented. Or the counselors might prefer to read a prayer, especially if that is the custom to which the campers are used in their own church and home observances. Some feel there is more "holiness" in specially prepared prayers than in the informal approach. In camps where heretofore there has been little overt worship observance, the first step (if counselors and campers alike are to feel secure) might be to read a brief selection or prayer.

When Campers Go A-questing

There is a wide variety of camps: private camps, church camps, agency camps, school camps. In some camps the living groups stay together all day, venturing out into the woods, finding a spot for building a shelter, planning their own menus, and even making their utensils. Other camps may let the campers choose from work groups or interest groups that cut across the living groups. (This practice, however, is probably more desirable for older youth groups than for young campers or the teens.) Thus more campers can have the experience of working and planning and playing together. Thus, too, there is provided a cross section of personalities and wider experience in making those social adjustments that result in a community feeling. With younger campers, the living group offers basic security, and probably most if not nearly all the camping experiences can take place in this small "family."

Some church camps that have not yet adopted completely the rustic motif offer interest areas for exploration. Groups elect to discuss and explore and work on problems in human relationships, and not just pit their skill against the natural world. Within these groups they work and do their own planning, just as they would if they were building something in the woods. And problems of personal adjustments similar to those encountered in outdoor projects do come up. Shelter-building and cook-outs have no corner on "stuff of life" adjustments that help build personalities and generate a community spirit. In fact, it may be many times harder to dig for truth than to dig the earth for tree-planting; and more difficult to carry on teamwork while discussing international relationships than while cooking an outdoor meal.

In all these daily adventures there may be high moments—of silent, shared wonder; of singing together some very familiar hymn; of saying together slowly and with new thoughtfulness a Scripture verse or a poem, even repeating it after the counselor if it is one the campers do not yet know. Conversations may lead to a reaching out of the spirit into mysteries as yet unfathomed.

Not only would these groups quest for new experiences as they wrestle with nature in the raw, or discover, or discuss; they would be concerned for others beyond the camp. No camp should allow itself to be an idyllic island apart from the rest of the world. Campers may use some of their newly learned skills in making gifts for others: for their families, for children in a hospital, for aged ones, or for their school or church back home. A Christmas tree in the summer may be loaded with gifts to be sent overseas. A Thanksgiving festival may be staged and gifts donated.

Some camps leave their camp grounds enriched in some specific way: an extended area cleared, a new shelter built, some new rustic equipment made, trees or flowers or shrubs planted. Eroded hills may be replanted, and the miracle of plant life taking hold, watched by the campers. A dedicatory service may be worked out to mark the gift.

Evening Activities

Evening "doings" of various kinds may be closed—or perhaps also begun—with a thankful moment, but only if the campers' mood calls for it. Never should a group be quieted down so that the words of a prayer may be said in accordance with the usual routine. If they are rollicking, boisterous, even obstreperous, let the campers play hard, let them have stunts and laugh uproariously, sing, express the fun honestly and exuberantly. To go through the motions of some religious observance when campers are not ready is to be dishonest and hypocritical ourselves and to train them in being so.

When the spirit is right, part of a spiritual may be sung or a prayer thought spoken. Or perhaps a fellowship circle or some other ceremonial may round out the day. One is ever amazed at the lightning-like rapidity with which campers can turn from ear-splitting laughter to sing thoughtfully for a few minutes, and then, it may be, to stand under the stars in utter hushfulness.

Dramas and story hours are looked forward to. If it is rainy, perhaps there will be a music fest. No formal worship plans need to be made for such occasions. Yet often—say if the message of a play has gone across—there is that quieting in the group that betokens real thinking, even something akin to prayer on somebody's part. The same thing may happen when a good story has been well told. Again, if the mood is right, and to do so would not seem a crude intrusion, a song may be started, or a familiar Scripture passage recited clearly; soon others will join in. A prayer from within the group, not by a leader standing apart, may lift the thoughts of all, especially if it is brief and natural and clearly heard.

Struggles and Disappointments, Too

All is not always sweet and lovely at camp. Problems may loom. Disappointments may sting. Tensions may flare. Fear may grip. At such times, we all feel a greater need for God—need for comfort, need for guidance so that we may face forward. Whatever the crisis, if it is faced as though God were already in the group, helping positively, it can be weathered.

More difficult than outward problems are the tensions that arise in human relationships. Jealousy may be eating into some camper's life like a cancer. In a camp set up on a fiercely competitive basis someone may be groveling deeper and deeper into feelings of inferiority. Fortunately, today more attention is being given to the quality of camp community life; and a wholesome, flexible, democratic system circumvents many personality flare-ups.

In one camp, set up on the old-time rigid "council" basis with an elected council and parliamentary procedure imposed, there was a general seething unrest among the campers and resentment that the wishes of the majority were not being heard. A break-up of the authoritarian shell of the council pattern and a simpler choosing on the part of each living-group of their representatives established a more camplike, democratic set-up. Whether difficulties are experienced by one or more individuals or by the camp as a whole, facing them honestly, straightforwardly, can provide the stuff of growth, and of worship.

Ordinary Times

This minute, there just might be a camper gazing out over the lake with a quiet look on his face; two buddies walking down a trail, or just sitting talking; a cabin group, tired but glowing with the day's achievements; a camper and a counselor walking along slowly together. Whether the words be brought to the surface or not, there can be a consciousness of a Friend who had a way of walking along with people.

Some Dangers in Planning for Worship in Camp

One danger is that camp leaders may schedule specified periods for "devotions" or "worship" (or—should they wish merely to hint at the idea—"quiet time," or "angelus," or "day's end," and the like) and consider their job done. Thus, any worship experiences would be —in the campers' own minds—set off as something apart from the rest of camp life, perhaps even as something not quite so natural as boating or cooking or any of their other activities. Campers might attend the set services with a feeling of duty. Let us hasten to say that few indeed are the camps in the writer's experience where this sort of practice obtains. There is more generally a vigorous effort to achieve "a consciousness of God in the daily routine," a natural relating of God to all phases of the camper's day. And when campers go back home they continue to relate spiritual matters to the rest of their lives.

There is serious question whether the division between "sacred" and "secular" in much scholarly writing today is healthy, or even valid. Strangely, some church camp leaders, perhaps "bending over backward" to avoid formal, set programs or sickly sentimental piosity, have all but omitted such practices as might inspire reverence or lead campers to bring to the fore in their minds the implicit idea of fellowship with God.

The other danger is that of importing into the camp scene outworn forms and practices, for lack of creative thinking and adventurous effort to find new ones more suitable for use in camps. Much has been written against making camps "Sunday schools in the open," even on Sundays. How ill-fitting, we say, when a young camping group plan a service identical with the ones they know back home; they even drape a table with a sheet, thinking it necessary to have a "worship setting," unaware of the whole vast cathedral all around them.

It is this danger of which we are most fearful as we offer here suggested worship aids. We are afraid that somebody, somewhere, will suddenly discover a certain poem or meditation, click his heels together, and stand up and "give" this piece, replete of course with hymns and Scripture to match. We are afraid lest somebody use something here in the place of first looking and listening to God.

Using Materials Such as Are Offered Here

As we said in the companion volume, *Spiritual Values in Camping,*[1] camping's big adventure ahead is to evolve indigenously and naturally such forms and materials of worship as belong in camp life. Actually, many of the selections have originated in camp. A number were written by campers or camp leaders. They may not be great poetry from the point of view of purely literary judgment. But they seem to "ring true" to the way one feels at camp. The hope is that these bits and pieces will touch off a spark in others so that they too will express themselves in their own natural ways.

Purposely, we have not arranged these selections into neat little "programs," with all the parts set down. In the first place, particularly with younger children, we would not make of worship a series of programs. Nor have we even suggested whether a certain idea would fit best at morning quiet time, at vespers, on Sunday, or when. These are nuggets, seed thoughts, sparks from a campfire. Groups of campers and leaders, feeling their own inner needs and recognizing what will best express their thoughts, will choose and plan and use them in their own way.

Probably the widest use for these materials may not be in the setting up of formal services. Rather, a counselor may first become familiar with some of the materials for the age level with which he works. A moment may come on a hike, or down by the waterfront, or at mealtime, or day's end, when he may wish to turn quickly to a certain poem or meditation or Scripture. The use will fit naturally into the conversation at just a needed time.

It takes more to make a camper than "what the well-dressed camper should wear." There is more to worship than outward forms and materials.

PART TWO

WITH YOUNGER CHILDREN

3

Worship Ways with Younger Campers

WHAT ARE LITTLE PEOPLE LIKE? First of all, they are like *people*. Each stands on his or her own two feet and looks out at the world through a pair of eyes and with a brain all his own. Each makes his own noise, and expresses his own impressions of this universe in which he finds himself. Perhaps most important for counselors to remember, each has his very own reasons for what he does and says and thinks, just as a grown-up counselor has his reasons.

Counselors are chosen, of course, for their understanding of, and their ability to guide, children at the age level involved. Some camps accept a mixture of ages, some have just one basic age span. Where there are campers of widely varying ages, there must be of necessity little camps within the bigger camp. If possible, children should be divided according to their grade in school; if that is not feasible or if the number of campers in each grade does not warrant such an arrangement, those in a two-year age span may be put together—say the six- and seven-year-olds; the eights and nines; the tens and elevens; the twelves and thirteens; and so on. Barring this, the primary age (grades

1, 2, and 3) might possibly form living groups; then the junior age (grades 4, 5, and 6). In a later section will be considered the characteristics and worship guidance of the young teens (grades 7, 8, and 9 or ages 12, 13, and 14).

Vast strides take place in growth, even in one year. In long-term camps especially (six weeks or longer), the campers have a more relaxed and richer total experience when they associate with their own peer groups and with counselors attuned to their particular wave length.

We cannot segregate a section of a youngster's life and call that his spiritual or religious side, or develop it apart from the rest of him. He is his whole self at all times. He brings that whole self to every minute of camp life. He can immerse himself as completely in a fascinating story well told around the fire, as when he dives into the lake. All counselors, therefore, are responsible for his worship guidance; for worship will likely take place at the most unpredictable moments as the camping day moves along its happy pace.

Let us take the smaller ones first. "Children" we might call them, for they are dependent in many ways. For the time of their stay at camp, the counselors become pseudo parents. Activity is the constant need of these young campers. Theirs is a muscle hunger that demands movement for growing. At first glance, their energy seems inexhaustible, but they do tire easily because their height is shooting up and growing takes strength, too. Minds reach out inquisitively and with startling clarity and profundity. They are interested particularly in life and the things about them, especially things that move! They are enjoying the adventure of learning to read; a new dimension for self-expression is becoming theirs. They collect anything; a boy's pockets are never big enough. They want to be liked by everybody; a word of criticism or disapproval hurts. They live in the immediate now; events of "long ago" have to be made to relive in the present; there is little understanding as to time spans of the past. But there is widening interest in the world around and in children everywhere.

Boys and girls who are a little older, the juniors, continue to enjoy being active, but they must have purposes of their own for what they do. Mentally, they are able to gather information and piece it together, think and reason about bigger problems than they could when they were younger. They can prolong interest longer; they can take upon themselves larger tasks that demand sustained attention and complete them. By now they have learned many interesting things about their physical world—about weather, stars, earth, their own bodies. History studies in school have given them heroes who touch off their own dreaming of what they want sometime to do and be. Theirs is a strong sense of right and wrong. They form gangs—boys' gangs, girls' groups. What those of their own age think of them often matters more than what adults think. They are learning to be dependable and they fulfill responsibilities; to be given recognition or symbols of achievement enhances their self-picture. Physical energy and curiosity make this a right age for acquiring many camping skills, giving lifelong at-homeness in woods and water and weather. The adventure spirit is strong.

Some Goals for Worship Guidance

Each camp will have its own goals for the entire program. Contributing to these goals, common to most camps, are the special purposes in worship guidance:

a) That growing boys and girls may continue to wonder and reach for understandings; that they be helped to listen in quiet prayer to the God who speaks in their hearts, and to think with Him about His wonderful world and the way He would have them live.

b) That there may grow in the awareness of each one a warm security, not only in the good world and its resources about them and in their friends and loved ones, but in God's love and protecting care as well; that they may wish to respond with thankful prayers and songs and thoughts; that during these years when they are becoming sensitive to changes and disruptions (some will have experienced drastic changes in their immediate lives already), the great laws of God are dependable and loving.

c) That the natural responsiveness of their hearts to beauty and kindness and love be nurtured so that they will continue to respond in this way; that thus a positive approach may be made that will heal and help individuals who have already become conditioned to unloving ways; and that habits may be deepened for expressing love to others near and far through surprises, through gifts, through financial support, and through service.

When?

In some camps there may be no definite periods set aside for worship in the whole camp or even in the living groups. In others, the daily schedule will include a gathering of the whole camp for worship, or perhaps the beginning of the day in each living group with worship.

In some camps there will be one or more rather special services. In church camps, perhaps two such services—

different in setting and purpose—would be held during the camp week.

Let it be pointed out quickly that in speaking of a service with children, we are not thinking of a formal pattern such as would be used with adults. All that is done would be within the thought forms and experience range of the youngsters. Probably *no* set service would be held with the younger ones, but rather plans would be made by the counselors for lifting to the worship level many high points through the days. Even with juniors, the form of a service would be quite simple and clear and the atmosphere would be relaxed. The gradual moving from fun-singing to a spiritual could possibly quiet campers' thoughts and bring readiness for talking with God. The content of their moments of worship would be drawn from the camp life: something to be shared by one of the living groups, perhaps; or something in nature for which thankfulness might be expressed; or a story showing a need about which the campers might wish, with God's help, to begin to do something; or even a problem in personal relations within the camp (not calling attention to individuals, of course), a general problem to be considered together so that with God's help, all might decide how to face it better. Most of the planned as well as the unplanned times of worship with boys and girls will be of the happy, wonder-awareness type, and much of the content will be thankfulness to the God who gives such wonders and gives us life and eyes and hearts to understand.

The older boys and girls can help plan and participate; again, counselors through some guiding conversations can lead them away from the patterns into which they might fall—hymn-Scripture-prayer-talk-or-story, etc.—into more natural, easy, personal expressions.

Before they are ready to plan, something must be felt first. Perhaps the counselors in their daily conversations might share little thoughts or questions that have come out spontaneously in the day's end talks with the campers; the worship counselor then might see if one of the groups would be ready to tell the whole camp, or another group, about its experience. "It takes a lot of living together before we have worship," remarked one counselor. He was right. As campers grow to feel more at home with one another, with their leaders, and with God, their worship will spring more naturally.

When Worship Comes

With counselors themselves attuned to campers and to the beautiful world and to its Maker, there will undoubtedly be high moments. Most likely, these will come in the living groups or discovery groups as they hobnob together during the day. In this intimate family fellowship, campers can be natural; they know they can express what they feel and the others will understand—or at least it *should* be that way.

No counselor need fear such moments, or feel awkward or wonder how to meet them. The moment will carry itself along; something a camper might say will be enough, and to add a word would take away the shine of the discovery. A counselor walking with a boy toward the dining area learned this lesson. A redbird suddenly flew across the path. In the faintest whisper the boy breathed, "Don't say a word . . . don't say a word," almost as if he feared grown-ups couldn't be trusted to be quiet. Another new camper, looking out on a freshly drenched earth that first morning, said, "Ain't God wonderful?"

In a group of wideawake campers of primary age, a "wonder list" of questions had been made at the beginning of a hike. Probably the campers were aware, with the counselor, that one hike would not provide all the answers; but the counselor suggested they might keep on thinking, and maybe look in some books when they got back. One camper queried, "Did God put all these wonderings in my mind?" And all were quiet for a few moments.

Several in another group would sing a little couplet used in a number of denominations, and when the others heard it, they wanted to learn it, too:

> Each little flower that opens,
> Each little bird that sings,
> He made their glowing colors,
> He made their tiny wings.[1]

The counselor, after a discussion of seasons and weather and some initial instruction to the juniors in weather-reading, quoted quietly Genesis 8:2, and Ecclesiastes 3:11. Some of the campers quoted the Scripture with her. In an early camp, one group planted bulbs, and by the box—even when all that was visible was the dark earth—they printed a card, "He hath made everything beautiful in its time." That was an act of faith!

The more experiences boys and girls have planting and tending something, the more they learn how to care for pets and farm animals, the more fully they experience partnership with an ever-creating God. The more fully, too, they can appreciate and express thankfulness for others who grow crops, care for forests, look after animals, etc. Thus, the work of people is understood as a part of the Father's care, as is the work of the plants and animals themselves in growing according to His plan. City children who may be pathetically underprivileged (even if rich economically) in awareness of sources of food, clothing, and shelter have their eyes and hearts opened at camp.

If there can be pets in camp or if visits to farms can bring the campers close to the birth-life-death cycle, a new dimension is added to their understanding of this greatest of all mysteries: life. In the tiniest forms of life is revealed a Plan. We can but be thankful to Him who is the source of all life; and we can live all our lives with more reverence for life.

Prayer is the heart of worship, whether in a close, informal little group of boys and girls or in a majestic congregation. Boys and girls learn to pray by praying—simply, easily, naturally, in their own way. Always the focus of attention is not on how to pray but rather upon the wonderful love of God, until we simply *want* to thank Him; or upon some need about which we wish to talk with Him. When milk and crackers are being given out in the evening the simple "Thank You, God, for milk and crackers" is enough. With some who may not have learned to stop and think of others and their needs, there may be a beginning prayer, "Help us remember to take turns in our work and in our play." In fact, a little tune might be put to it, so that the prayer is sung by all the campers. Ten- and eleven-year-old boys and girls will be able to say more thoughts at a time in prayer, and to think their own prayers silently, too, as well as sing them. When old enough to discuss and realize the meaning of the Lord's Prayer, the older boys and girls can pray it at times when they are ready.

Loving thoughts are in a real sense a prayer. Boys and girls may want to pray, before they go to sleep at night, "And, loving Father of us all, please protect and bless our parents and brothers and sisters . . . and pets, etc." Only through inner feeling is the truth of Samuel Coleridge's definition of prayer learned:

> He prayeth best who loveth best,
> All things both great and small;
> For the dear God who loveth us,
> He made and loveth all.[2]

Counselors should be careful about thoughts implanted in little campers' minds the last thing before they go to sleep. To rest in a warm realization of God's love and tender care, and to thrill to the fact that "He has given us all things richly to enjoy," is more healthful for spiritual growth (and for quiet sleep) than the concept of "if I should die," or of a God who "takes," a fearsome picture for which young minds are not ready. The couplet which the reader will recognize from this reference came out of a day of stern, loveless theology picturing God as angry judge rather than loving Father-heart. In fact, too little attention through the centuries has been given the love of God; writings that bring out this aspect are scant. Maybe that is the basic reason why man acts so unloving, both to God and to neighbor. Little boys and girls, in their tender impressionable years, can experience profoundly the loving-kindness of God, and there will be within them a limitless reservoir of love as they grow.

In some faiths and sects, the thought of God is expanded from the Father-concept to include the Mother-concept as well. In some, the adherents pray to Father-Mother God. In some faiths the feminine being who gave birth to God's son is thought of as actively interceding for people today. Whatever the pictures in people's thoughts, there is an overarching truth that God's love expresses all the best we have ever known in Father-Mother love, infinitely multiplied.

Any conversations about prayer with campers should help them feel God is not far away, and that they can think and speak the natural thoughts they have in the most natural ways. The important thing is to mean what one prays. The author of the following poem is unknown, but it might have come from a camp:

> To say my prayers is not to pray
> Unless I mean the words I say;
> Unless I think to whom I speak
> And with my heart His blessing seek.
> Then let me, when I come to pray,
> Not only heed the words I say,
> But let me seek with earnest care
> To have my thoughts go with my prayer.[3]

Sometimes counselors may help sharpen a camper's ideas of prayer by questions. "When we pray that everything may go our way, are we praying in the right spirit?" One counselor described two situations: in one, a camper held back, hesitating to participate in woods exploring or swimming for fear he might get poison ivy or something else might happen to him; in the other, a camper learned what he could about avoiding dangers, then joined with the group happily to learn more about God's universe and how to live in it. "Which," the counselor asked, "would feel closer to God when he prayed?" Two campers in the same cabin were saying their good-night prayers. One asked God for a number of things for himself, including care through the night. The other thanked God for so many gifts, and prayed for others as well as for himself. Which one showed more of God's love through his prayer?

Nature's treasure chest offers never ending opportunities for discovering, for discussing, and, at times, for becoming more aware, possibly, for praying. A group found a bird's nest no longer in use, and tried taking it apart to see what it was made of. "Can you put it back together again?" someone asked. All were silent. A thought deeper than could have been put into words was going through young minds: *How* do birds know just how to build like this?

Some junior campers were learning about insects. Do they *all* bite? Why do some bite? Did God create them just to annoy animals and people? Which ones get along in the same surroundings? Which ones are commercially useful? Which ones are used for food among some primitive peoples? What animals depend largely upon insects for food? What insects depend on one another? What plants depend on insects for pollenization? It happened that there was in the camp a young man who had made a special study of insects. He helped the campers see the amazing balance in nature and showed them what sometimes happens when man changes God's arrangement and introduces insects into different regions from their original habitat. He told of some experiments he himself was conducting, trying to get rid of certain insects in his garden by using the balance-of-nature principle (planting alongside an item upon which a certain insect preyed another item on which another insect preyed which would take care of the first one!) rather than through dangerous insecticides. That night in the cabin groups came many spontaneous expressions of wonder at God's plan, and desire to find out more about it.

Every camp has its own peculiar natural world; and as campers find more of the secrets of that bit of nature, their wonder and worship will grow. One camp had more rocks than anything else. But the deeper the campers delved into the secrets of rocks the more exciting became the story. They reenacted what they thought might have been scenes of some thousands of years ago, as told by the rocks.

Even little campers can tell the difference when man uses nature's resources as he should, and when he despoils and abuses. Practices of soil conservation can be observed on the grounds of the camp itself; in turn, when campers go back home they can influence their parents and friends—for example, to make compost heaps of leaves rather than burning them; to plant sloping hills with rooting vines or bushes or grass. Thus in helping to save or heal hurt places on the earth, they are working with God as truly as when they plant and grow things. They can readily understand that one does not merely ask God to keep floods from coming, one does one's share to be sure floods are not caused.

Likewise, discussion of weather can lead to more mature ideas of prayer. Does one pray for the kind of weather *he* wants, regardless of the needs of the farmers? Is that kind of prayer in the spirit God would want us to have? Is it not good to know that God is dependable? The fault of people in creating the conditions that cause wind storms can be discussed. Rainy days may be made particularly enjoyable in camp, not only by opening rainy day chests, but also by rejoicing in rain as a good gift and as a part of the big balance and Plan. Cook-outs and sleep-outs that bring campers into ways of working more closely with nature can also be times for quiet conversations that lead to deeper securities in God.

As Campers Learn Better to Pray and Worship

Generally, the approach to prayer and worship with children is through simple conversations, then perhaps quiet or a prayer; sometimes there may be a Scripture verse that says the very thoughts they are thinking. *Never* would a device so adult and so mechanical as "sentence prayers" be used by the counselor. In fact, the counselor should not be too concerned to have words spoken aloud by campers in prayer; after all, real praying is for the ear of One Above. The deeper concern of the counselor is that worship be from the inside. It will come out in ways native to children. It should not be forced into stilted grown-up patterns ever.

Conversations may bring out "things we've seen today that have showed ways God loves us," and then the group may decide upon a "Thank You" refrain, such as, "For these things we thank You, O God." As the counselor repeats each evidence of God's love that has been mentioned by the campers, the whole group prays, "For these things we thank You, O God." Thus, a litany is built but no word has been mentioned about "building a litany." Rather, they have simply let their thankful thoughts come forth into this form. Always the form is subordinate to the feeling.

Some camps put into the hands of their junior campers little daily guides to be used in some morning quiet time, perhaps in the living groups or by the boy or girl alone. For example, when he is old enough to read easily, he may find a suggestion, "Close your eyes and think of some of the most wonderful and great things you've ever seen, and write them down here. Then, close your eyes again and thank God for creating such a world. Maybe you'll wish to ask Him to be your best." Or on another page of the devotional booklet may be a Scripture passage, or a poem about growing things; and the camper will think of many things that have small beginnings, and ask God's help in beginning some good thoughts that might grow in his own life.

Probably in every camp there should be some attention to daily bread as God's gift; and some thought about persons who go to bed hungry every day. Junior boys and girls might want to plan a special meal when they would eat less and give some money to buy food for people hungry far away. In many camps there have been discovery groups on "our daily bread" in which they consider how wheat and corn and rye are grown, transported, baked into breadstuffs, distributed.

The planning of gifts for others, both at and away from the camp, touches springs of love in young hearts. Some may use newly learned skills and craftsmanship in fashioning gifts for family and friends. When the handiwork is exhibited, perhaps there might be a prayer that all the work of our hands will be a way of showing God how we thank Him for making us so we can make things, and a way of showing our love to others.

There may come times when a camper has hurt another and needs to find courage to ask God's forgiveness and the other camper's forgiveness. Counselors can help them make this honest, hard step so that all their lives they will be the stronger. Discussions of choices that have to be made in the camp, and back home in daily living, may cause campers to feel the need of continuing to ask God to help them be strong and true.

Aids

Since most of the younger campers' experiences of prayer and worship will grow thus informally, and unpredictably, the counselor may well just keep his own mind and heart attuned and ready. He may have read through, perhaps several times, the resources offered in this book. He will be the more apt, then, to think of an idea that will help. Or perhaps, he might turn to what he needs at the time. Counselors working with ten- and eleven-year-old boys and girls in planning for special services may discuss with them what would help the group worship; they themselves can help select from resources such as these. Or something here may cause a camper to think of something similar in his own experience—and he will share *that*.

Little boys and girls love to sing, and increasingly there are available songbooks with nature songs and fun songs and motion songs and all kinds of selections suitable for camps. Many of the folk songs of the nations of the world are not beyond youngsters' singing; and through the singing a bond of kinship is forged early. One of the finest resources to have in a camp is a person of another race or nationality, who is there to live with the campers and help all feel the basic kinship of peoples everywhere.

A few simple hymns may be used by the juniors in their worship services; these should be chosen with care to express loving thoughts of God. The music counselor can bring delightful records, such as bird calls that, more eloquently than any human words, will bid for awareness and perhaps lead to worship. Even younger boys and girls can awaken to the haunting beauty of good songs and recordings. With these boys and girls a few worship-responses may be learned and sung. Children are marvelously creative and can put tunes to thoughts they are thinking, making their own songs. The music counselor can write them on a music staff, and the whole camp can learn. Probably nothing as formal as a hymnal would be needed in camp. The words of a few choice hymns can be printed with black crayon in large letters on rolls of white paper, and illustrated by the campers. In teaching a new hymn, the counselor plays or sings it first, so that campers can get the "feel" of it.

What of aids for the eye? Pictures have a place at camp as elsewhere in all work with children. Illustrated books in which boys and girls can identify butterflies or rocks, or whatever, are in order. But probably few if any pictures will be needed as aids to worship. Nature itself provides a pageant of pictures. Ordinarily films are not recommended for camps, but certain ones for younger boys and girls might bring to them friends across the world and deepen their sense of the human community, or might open up for them some of nature's wonders in addition to those they are discovering at camp. *Days of Wonder* (a filmstrip with recording, obtainable from denominational publishing houses or from the National Council of Churches) depicts a boy and girl finding for themselves some of the seasons' wonders; the refrain "All Thy People Praise Thee" weaves a worship feeling throughout the film.

Stories also belong with younger campers, in camp as elsewhere. The right stories can lead to the threshold of worship. But *not* the obvious-moral kind! Campers are bright. They will recognize the propaganda, no matter how cleverly it is disguised. Stories of real people who have done brave things for God and for others will speak for themselves. Those people lived. They dared. They suffered, perhaps. The storyteller does not need to suggest that they were heroic; the campers will know.

The secret of good storytelling is to feel and see the plot clearly, and tell it simply. The hearers can fashion their own feelings, for in that is their participation. Vicarious experiencing prepares them for a closing worship prayer or maybe to think for a moment in silence when the last word of the storyteller has died away.

How should we prepare for a story such as might be used around the campfire some evening or on a Sunday morning? First, let it be a *live* story, one that grips the counselor as he reads. Let the counselor surrender to the excitement of it, going over the details until he knows the progression. Then possibly he might practice on the trees, visualizing the events as though they were in technicolor before his eyes. Campers will then see and feel, too.

When a story is to be used to lead to worship, it has to be that kind of story; then the setting should be right. The campfire glow is a good setting. If the story is told indoors, lights may be dimmed or there might be candleglow or lantern-light. And *not too much* should be said. Singing might prepare. A prayer might follow—if the feeling is right.

Campers' own acting-out of stories can also be useful in worship, and their choral reading or group reading can help them recreate scenes in imagination. Campers can make their own dramatic versions of ideas that are real to them; afterward, they can express their own new purposes in prayer.

The realization of the goals of worship guidance of younger campers may come much later in their lives; but camp can help set their feet along the path of gladness in God's love, and of naturalness in praying and in expressing love, too. "God, there are so many ways of thanking you!" breathed by a camper, revealed that she was growing in her awareness of the myriads of ways—and yet the ease—for praying and worshiping.

4

Finding God through Beauty and through His Plan for Providing for All

GOD'S LOVE

We do not see the wind,
  We only hear it sigh.
It makes the grasses bend
  Whenever it goes by.

We do not see God's love,
  But in our hearts we know
He watches over us
  Wherever we may go.

We do not have to see
  To know the wind is here;
We do not have to see
  To know God's love is near.[1]

WHERE SHALL WE FIND GOD?

God is in all beautiful things.
We can go out in the woods and find him
If we will rest and be quiet and think;

And if we are lonely and sad,
He will fill us with joy.

And God is nearer than this.
We can go into our homes and find him
Where fathers and mothers are working
To care for their children.

And God is in cities and towns,
We can go into the streets and find him,
Where people are helping each other,
Helping lost children and finding them homes,
Nursing sick sailors on hospital boats.
God's love is in people.

God is in us, making us helpful,
Giving us strength to be kind and do right.

God is a Spirit, a Spirit of love,
A Spirit of truth, of kindness, of joy.
Wherever these are,
We find God.[2]

WHERE DO YOU FIND GOD?

I find God in the rosy dawn
  That wakes me from my sleep:
For just a moment, in my bed,
Some loving "thank you" words are said
  As I awake from sleep.

I find God in my work and play
  At times I stop to think:
Good times full of love and cheer
Help me know that God is near,
  If I stop to think.

Evening, when the day is done,
Makes me think of God:
When I have tried to do my part,
My thoughts are happy, and my heart
Is glad to think of God.[3]

COUNTLESS WONDERS OF OUR GOD

Sky so bright,
Blue and light,
Stars how many hast thou?
Countless stars!
Countless times shall God
be praised now!

Forest green,
Cool, serene,
Leaves how many hast thou?
Countless leaves!
Countless times shall God
be praised now!

Deepest sea,
Wide and free,
Waves how many hast thou?
Countless waves!
Countless times shall God
be praised now!

Eternity,
Eternity,
Hours how many hast thou?
Countless hours!
Countless times shall God
be praised now![4]

ANTIPHONAL

Leader: I wonder how flowers come from seeds.
I wonder how God made the earth.
I wonder how God made the sea.

Response: "Great things doeth he which we cannot comprehend."

Leader: I wonder how worms can spin cocoons.
I wonder how worms can turn into butterflies.
I wonder how bees can make honey.

Response: "Great things doeth he which we cannot comprehend."

Leader: I wonder how birds can build their nests.
I wonder how day turns into night.
I wonder where flowers go in the fall.

Response: "Great things doeth he which we cannot comprehend."

Leader: I so often wonder
About so many things—
The colors in the flowers,
The way the robin sings,
The way the moon lights up the sky,
The sun that makes the day,
The stir of things,
The whirr of wings,
The velvet butterfly,
And so I go on wondering—
But now,
I give my thanks and sing
To God the great Creator
Of every lovely thing.[5]

GOD GAVE ME EYES

God gave me eyes that I might see
The wonder of a blossoming tree,
My dolly's face, my story book
And how the various creatures look.

God gave me ears that I might hear
The laugh of brooklets ringing clear,
My kitten's purr, a violin
And Mother, when she calls me in.

God gave a nose that I might learn
The perfume of each flower in turn,
Of fragrant foods prepared to eat,
The dusty smell of new cut wheat.

God gave a tongue that I might know
The flavor of all fruits that grow,
The taste of honey from the bee,
And good things Mother cooks for me.

God gave a sense of touch that I
Might do my work, feel wind pass by,
Might know the sun's caressing heat
And dusty roads beneath my feet.

I thank You, God, for making me
So that I hear and feel and see;
And since these dear gifts came from You
I'll use them as You'd want me to.[6]

MIRACLES

The world is full of miracles,
Of that I am sure.
But, you ask

What is a miracle?
That depends,
That depends on what you call a miracle.
I think a miracle is a wonder—
It is God at work.
So it was with the ancients.
"There is Something beyond the power of man," they said.
They saw Him at work.
Ways of explaining things have changed;
Science has given new answers to men's questions.
Yet God is still at work;
There are still miracles.

The sunrise is a miracle.
Darkness fades,
The early morning light makes mountain mists lavender
And the eastern sky rosy and gold.
We know about the solar system
But sunrise is still a miracle.[7]

THINKING WHAT A "MIRACLE" IS

It is a miracle
When dead leaves fall from a tree and bury deep in the earth and make it rich for other plants and trees.
It is a miracle—
That seeds and bulbs know when it is time to wake up and push through the ground.
It is a miracle—
That birds know when to fly south and when to come back again.
It is a miracle—
That each year we can be sure of these things.

Prayer: O God, we thank you for your miracles of growth and change. We are glad that we can depend on these miracles happening every year. We thank you for the miracle of our minds that can think lovely thoughts. O God, we thank you! Amen.[8]

SOME LOVELY THINGS

I saw some lovely things today;
I feel, dear God, I'd like to pray.
I saw some tiny, little things—
Some humming birds with gauzy wings,
A flower with its head held high
As though its blue came from the sky.
I saw some lovely things today;
I feel, dear God, I'd like to pray.

I heard some wondrous things today;
I feel, dear God, I'd like to pray.
I heard a brook; it seemed to me
To catch the rhythm of the sea,
I heard a bird; it sang to me
A joyous, lilting melody.
I heard some wondrous things today;
I feel, dear God, I'd like to pray.

Perhaps, dear God, the woodland air
Was really breathing out a prayer—
  The prayer I prayed.
The awe and wonder in my heart
Were such a very vital part
  Of what is truest prayer.[9]

MINE FOR DISCOVERING

I own the mountain's purple tints,
The sunset through my pine;

A bird song in my apple tree
Is priceless, yet to me 'tis free—
The universe is mine.[10]

GOD'S MUSIC EVERYWHERE

God is making music.
If you listen you can hear;
His voice is in the gentle wind
That stirs the willow tree:
He is singing in the brook
That wends its way to sea.
He's playing chords of harmony
Upon the mighty deep,
The evening stars are notes divine
That lull the world to sleep.[11]

WATCHING HOW A ROBIN MAKES HER NEST

Has a Robin "intelligence"? Is it a *planned* job, from the site selection to the final lining? What comes before the mud cup is made? How is the cup made and shaped? How long need it dry? What next? How long from start of nest to first egg? How many nests a season? Does father sit and brood eggs? Do both feed the young? [12]

SOME OF GOD'S PLANS

THESE show us God's plans for plants:

Seeds flying in the wind, sailing on the water, sticking to animals and people, carried by the birds, to find new homes.

Seeds lying safe from the cold under the blanket of snow.

Plants sprouting and growing when the sun warms, the showers water and the soil feeds them.

Flowers attracting bees with bright colors and sweet smells.
Bees coming for honey and leaving pollen to make new seeds.
Great and wonderful are thy works, O Lord God!

THESE show us God's plans for animals:
Foxes growing thick coats of fur to keep them warm.
Dogs finding their way home.
Squirrels storing up nuts for winter.
Bears crawling into caves and sleeping through the cold weather.
Birds starting on their long journey south.
Dogs working with men to draw sleds, tend sheep, lead blind people.
Great and wonderful are thy works, O Lord God!

THESE show us God's plans for people:
The farmer raising corn, wheat, vegetables for food.
Cows giving milk, sheep growing wool, horses carrying loads.
Miners digging coal to keep people warm.
Children having fun in the snow.
People painting pictures, playing music, writing poems.
People using their minds to think and their hands to work.
People everywhere thinking and working with other people to make the world better and happier.
Great and wonderful are thy works, O Lord God! [13]

GOD'S LOVE IS EVERYWHERE

I look out from my window
And see the budding trees,
Whose lovely lacy branches
Are waving in the breeze;

I see the grass upspringing,
And flowers bright and fair,
And then I feel like singing,
"God's love is ev'rywhere!"

'Tis God our heav'nly Father,
Who made the world so fair,
His love is all around us,
We're always in His care;
I hear the bird songs ringing
Out on the morning air
And I, too, feel like singing
"God's love is ev'rywhere!" [14]

THE EARTH IS FULL OF THY RICHES

Deep under plain and mountain lie
  Bright riches folded in;
Silver and gold the hillsides hold,
  Iron, and brass, and tin,
Copper and oil, far out of sight,
And coal, and jewels full of light.

Down under field and garden wait,
  Silently, seeds and roots,
They will be flowers, soon or late;
  They will be grass and fruits;
And where an acorn sleeps may come
A tall green tree to bless a home.

Far down the lovely waters rise;
  Their quiet way they make
Into the light, all sparkling bright,
  Fountain, and brook and lake,
Clear cooling streams, deep wells, and springs—
The earth is full of God's good things! [15]

GOD KNOWS JUST WHAT WE NEED

Matthew 6:8

"How does a mother bird know just how to build a nest?"

(Campers may, in this conversation, tell about some *different* kinds of nests and some of the materials the mother bird needs to put into the nest. How does she find these needed materials? She seems to just know where to go; and after she gets what she needs, she puts the parts together so carefully and painstakingly, as if she had a design in her head to work from.)

"When the baby birds come, how does the mother bird know how to take care of them?"

(Campers may venture their own thoughts as to how she "knows" and may tell about discoveries they have made of eggs or of baby birds being fed in their nests or being taught to fly. Soon one will suggest that God has planned for the birds, and for every living thing. Somehow, not in words such as humans use, but in some way, He tells them what to do. Little squirrels store up nuts for the long winter time when there will not be food to be found. Are there other evidences of God's care over little creatures?)

"It makes us feel warm and thankful inside when we think of the way God cares for birds and creatures. We, too, are His creatures. He plans for us. He gives us homes and mothers and fathers who provide food and love for us. And He helps us grow very strong and sturdy so that we can begin to help, too. He knows just what we need."

Moment for wondering silent thought. "Thank You for loving us, God!" [16]

GOD'S LOVE 'ROUND ABOUT US AT CAMP

Genesis 8:22

"What has made us glad today?"

(The counselor's question, spoken softly and a bit casually, may touch off a bit of thinking, and a camper will be sure to have some "glad thing" to share right off. Maybe it is the feeling of a soft bed to rest in after the busy time of the camp day; maybe it is the fun of waking up in the morning with the sun very bright and a whole new day to be camped in; maybe it is having a "cabin family" all together, liking each other and having conversations such as this. Or perchance one after another will remember some special "discovery"—a scene "just like a picture" that campers gathered to view when called by one; a flower never noticed before, but looked up and welcomed then by name from the book as a new friend; or some new skill begun or "just about" learned . . . what joy to think of "glad moments" together before going to sleep.)

"God gives us these things to discover."

"He gives us, too, minds to reach out and ask questions and feet to go exploring and hands to reach and draw and make things and to help one another."

"Things might have been all one color, of course, but God put a bit of special love into making them beautiful. Can we list some colorful things seen today?"

"Sounds identify things in our world, and there are sounds of beauty like music. Can we list some happy sounds?"

O God, how You must love us! Thank You for everything glad.[17]

FORECASTING

The campers were gathered in the lodge awaiting the daily weather forecast. Then they would know better how to plan, what to take to their various family-group shelters.

The voice came on the radio, pleasant, genial. "Good travel weather today," the weatherman said. "Winds to northeast, temperatures in the middle seventies. Keep tuned to this station for further developments. A cool wave is moving this way from the Midwest."

"But how?" queried Jackie, who was always finding something new to wonder about. And she was always asking. "I mean, how can that fellow on the radio always know for sure what the weather is going to do?"

Robin, a counselor, was standing near. "Well, maybe he doesn't always know for dead sure," she responded thoughtfully, "but usually he can tell very definitely. You see, the weather forecasters have to study carefully. They learn about trade winds and currents and meteorology. They find that certain laws seem to be in operation in regard to weather, just as 'laws' govern tides and the circulation of our blood and the moisture cycle and the seasons. The forecaster has special maps. He gets news from all sections as to prevailing winds and temperatures. He knows in what direction storms or hurricanes are moving. Sensitive instruments tell him what the pressures are, and the humidity in the air. He puts it all together and tells us what he finds."

"Then it's not just a whim or guess every day," Jackie put in. Then, with a new wondering thought, "You mean that God sets it all up and it works by laws we can depend upon?"

"Yes," answered Robin quietly. "We should not pray

for God to change weather just for our whims. Let's look up Matthew 5:45b." [18]

WHETHER THE WEATHER . . .

Monty was weather and compass man at camp. He liked to have campers to crowd around and watch him make readings about the humidity and barometric pressure and other indications. Nothing pleased him more than to have a camper volunteer to learn, and then take a reading very carefully, for it must be just right.

Jane did not know much about weather and such things. She showed what a "tenderfoot" she was as she stepped out of her cabin one morning and remarked, "Oh, how wet this grass is! Must've rained last night." "Can't you see it didn't, you silly?" scoffed Jerry. The sun was shining, mockingly. "How come it's wet, then?" she asked triumphantly. "Guess we'd better check with Monty," answered Jerry, who didn't feel quite ready with the answer himself.

Monty smiled. "You see," he said, just as if they were grown-up and informed people who *did* see, "there is always some moisture in the air; it isn't visible to our eyes, of course. But the instruments can tell. When warm air containing the water vapor comes in contact with something cool, the vapor changes to drops of water. That's why grass and flowers are damp; they are cool, down close to the ground. We call the condensation 'dew.' Breathe against a mirror yourself. It is cool; your breath has moisture and is warm. Drops begin to form on the mirror." Jane and Jerry felt very informed as they danced along the path to breakfast with Monty.

"I wish the sparkle would last all day," Jane said wistfully. "The moisture cycle has its work to do just as we do," quietly observed Monty. "Tell you what: after breakfast, let's look up Ecclesiastes 1:7 and talk about it some more." [19]

WONDERING ABOUT ROCKS AND LONG AGO

Vicki and Rory were going with their parents and their grandmother on a long train ride. They jumped up and down at the wonder and glory of it all. Places they had never been before, sights they had never seen before.

Little did they realize what they *would* see in California. But the most special thing they saw was on the way back. The big train stopped one morning, and all the people got off to spend the whole day on the edge of the biggest, farthest, most beautifully colored pile of large mountainous rocks Vicki and Rory had ever seen —the Grand Canyon!

That afternoon, the bus on which they rode around the rim of the canyon stopped, and they visited with the forest ranger in a little rustic hut. Standing there on the porch, looking out over the beautiful, changing colors of the tall peaks ranging back as far as the eye could see, they caught their breath in wonder. But there was a low note of wonder in the ranger's voice, too, that afternoon. "People have learned how to 'read' the message in the rocks," he said. "They tell us about how many hundreds of years ago that rock became as it is now." Then he paused. People began to imagine, 'way back, many, many hundreds of years, many thousands of years, many billions of years. "And down at the very bottom of the gorge," said the ranger quietly, "is that strange utterly black lifeless rock, the beginning of all things—*before* life as we know it existed on this earth."

"In the beginning, God . . ." said someone softly. Everyone was very quiet.[20]

GOD'S PLAN FOR MOTHERS AND FATHERS

"He careth for you." I Peter 5:7b.

(*Note:* this is a simple, not-too-serious conversation that may open possibilities for campers to ask easily about the facts of life and love; there should not be on the part of the counselor an air of this being something strange and difficult to talk about. Let this kind of conversation be as natural and loving and simple and to the point as all little conversations; and let it be in a warm atmosphere of thankfulness to God for His plan.)

"What baby creatures have we discovered here at camp?"

(Campers might recall some and tell a little about them and about what their "parents" do for them.)

"What other baby creatures do we know?"

(Some may know about little creatures that have a protective camouflaging coat that distinguishes them not at all from the surrounding woods until they are grown strong enough to take care of themselves.)

"What kinds of food do they need?"

(Soon the discussion may lead to a warm awareness that somehow mothers *know*, from some deep feeling inside them, that they should get this or that kind of food for their young; that they should do this or that—like the rabbit making a blanket for little rabbitkin.)

"God has special plans for all his creatures. He teaches them this deep feeling as to what they should do; he helps them love their babies and want to care for them. Mother birds feed their babies worms. Mother bumblebees make bee bread for their little ones. Each creature seems to know what the young most need.

"It is God's plan, too, that when grown-up creatures love one another very unselfishly with their whole bodies, the young get started and begin to grow. After a while, they are grown enough. Some creatures are in eggs, like the baby chicken or bird; it has to peck through and then it is strong enough to walk out upon earth. Little human babies have to grow a long time before they are ready to be born—about nine months. The father's body has a place where many little sperm cells grow. He has an organ that sends these into the body of the mother when he loves her very, very much. She has an opening meant to receive them. The father's sperm cells work their way up into passages leading to the place the mother's egg comes from. One of the father's cells, meeting the egg the mother's body has made, joins it—and a new life starts to be. Of course, the egg is not always where the sperm cell can reach it. The mother's body has room for the new life to grow; and it is nourished by her body in a safe, warm, soft place until it is ready to be born, after nine months. During this time, she and the father have time to prepare for the joyful coming of the baby. Because they love each other so much, they are ready to love it very much. Babies, even from the first hours after birth, seem to *know* if they are loved; they grow more happily when they are.

"This sounds like wonderful magic . . . it is God's special plan. From a little seed-cell the tall pine tree grows. From a mere speck of an egg laid on a leaf a caterpillar and then a butterfly will grow. From a beginning germ of life will come a huge elephant.

"Shall we pause and thank God for His plan?"

"O God, You loved us so much. We're glad to be

alive. We're glad to know of Your plan for all living things. May we live happy, clean lives to show You how thankful we are." [21]

LITTLE HOUSES

A house that grows in the meadow
With walls that are soft and sweet,
Is nice for a caterpillar
When he needs a bite to eat.

A house that is made of bubbles
Feels good to the tender skin
Of each little bubble blower
When he safely hides within.

A house so cleverly woven
With silk that is new and strong,
Will do for the baby spiders—
But it's not where I belong.

Each little house is different,
Each one as snug as can be,
But none are quite so cozy
As my little house for me! [22]

After campers have built themselves a "shelter" in the woods, and feel it is their very own, they may enjoy thinking of shelters or homes of other creatures and see how many they can describe or draw. Resting from fixing up their own shelter, or their cabin, they might say the little poem above and a thank-you prayer to God the Father who plans so that the creatures can have just the kind of houses they need. Quietly the campers might remember people who do not have a cozy home, and pray for them.

5

We Learn to Pray and Trust His Care

AN EXTRA PRAYER

Sometimes I say an extra prayer,
Besides the one for which I kneel.
I stand and look up at the stars,
And tell our Father how I feel.
I do not ask for anything;
I just feel happy thro' and thro'.
I let my heart give thanks and sing
Till all the world seems good and true.[1]

WE THANK THEE, LORD MOST HIGH

A group of boys and girls were discovering some of the wonderful things in the universe, the planets and the orderly way in which they move around the sun, the stars and how far the sky stretches into space. They learned of men who have used the telescope and other instruments to find out more about the universe. They found butterflies and moths and other insects which move from flower to flower carrying the tiny pollen grains, some of which these boys and girls saw through a microscope. They saw different parts of a flower and learned about the way in which a new seed is formed. The last day they met together, they wrote a prayer about the things they had discovered. This is what they wrote:

For the stars that shine in the night,
For the sun that gives heat and light,
We thank thee, Lord most high.

For all the birds with their beautiful wings,
For all the scientists who discover new things,
We thank thee, Lord, most high.

For the insects that scatter pollen to make more seeds,
For lakes, for trees, for grass, for weeds,
We thank thee, Lord, most high.

For plants that grow from seed to flower,
For Thy great love and helpful power,
We thank thee, Lord, most high.
Amen [2]

WHEN I'VE DONE WRONG

Dear God,
All wise and loving, too,
I come to tell You
Of the wrong I've done.
I did not want to do it, God,
I don't know why I did.
I feel ashamed and sorry, God,
About the wrong I've done.
I know that You are sorry, too,
And wish that I'd been strong.
Forgive me, God;
I know You will,

Because You understand
And love me
Even when I am not strong.
But I would be
The sort of child
Upon whom You
Depend.
You'll help me, God—
I know You will—
To make the words I say,
And all the things
I think about,
And all the things
I do
The sort of words
And thoughts and deeds
That bring me
Close to You. Amen.[3]

WHEN I DO NOT UNDERSTAND

There are so many things, dear God,
That I can't understand!
Why is it there are droughts and floods
And storms upon the sea?
Why is it that the brooks run dry
And little flowers die of thirst?
Why is it that some boys and girls
Are always hungry, never warm?
I think You know the reason why
These things are just the way they are.
I wonder—will You help me, God,
To understand them, too?
I wonder—can I help You, God,

Some day when I am wise,
To stop the droughts and storms and floods
And give all children food? [4]

GOD PLANNED ALL THINGS

Do the things which we call our own really belong to us? How did we get them? Where did they come from? Who owned them before they became ours?

To find the answers to these questions, let us go back to the very beginning of the world. We must think of that time when there was no world at all—only God and his great plan for the world he was to create.

No one knows just what God thought as he began to plan his world. But how carefully he made his plans for the gifts he would give to his children! He thought of the light and the darkness, the earth and the seas and the sky. He thought of the sun with its light and its heat. He thought of the moon and of the stars which shine like flickering candle lights in the dark blue sky of night.

God thought of living, growing things, too. He thought of grasses and plants and trees. He planned ways in which they would grow their own seeds to be planted year after year. He thought of animals and birds and fish of every kind. He planned wonderful ways in which their babies would be born so there would always be animals and birds and fish in his world. God was planning for a world that would go on and on.

Have you ever thought of how great God's plan of creation really was? Look around you and see how many things you are enjoying today because of God's plan for his world. If it is wintertime and you are sitting in your living room . . . you are being warmed by the burning of coal or gas, oil or wood taken from God's rich storehouse. These may have taken millions of years to form, but they are a part of God's plan for his world.

The wooden furniture in your room also came from God's world. It was once a part of the trees of God's creation. Your house, itself, is built of wood or stone, of brick or stucco. These materials came from the forest or they were made of clay and sand from the earth. If your room is lighted with electricity, that form of energy has been in the world from its beginning. Any metal in the room—a lamp, your light fixtures, radiator, door knobs—is all made of ores taken from mines in the earth. *Everything that you see in the room about you came from some substance planned by God in the creation of the world.*

The writer of one of the Psalms was probably looking around him one day when he, too, discovered that everything in the world came from God.

"God planned for and created the earth and everything in it," he thought. "God created the world and the men and women and boys and girls who live in it. So the earth and everything that it produces, the world and the people living in the world all belong to God."

Then with wonder in his voice, he cried:

"The earth is the Lord's,
And the fullness thereof;
The world, and they that dwell therein."
(Psalm 24:1.) [5]

6

We Work with God in Loving All and in Being His Helpers

HE WATCHES O'ER THE CHILDREN

All the little children,
Wherever they may be
In this land of sunshine
From sea to shining sea,
Have a loving Father
Who with tender care
Watches o'er the children
Here and everywhere.[1]

GOD'S LOVE

God's love must be in all the earth,
In earth, in sea, in air—
The sunshine lights the flowers and trees,
His wind blows through my hair.
God, let Your love be in my thoughts
And I'll send it everywhere! [2]

ALL THE WORLD IS GOD'S WORLD

All the world is God's world,
So we kneel and pray,
"Bless the other children,
Far and far away!

"When our sun is shining,
And our land is bright,
Their land's in the shadow,
Keep them through the night.

"When our day is over,
And our twilight comes,
They are seeing sunrise.
Bless them in their homes!"

Long the miles between us;
Though we cannot call
Over seas and mountains,
God will bless us all! [3]

ONE FRIENDLY NEIGHBORHOOD

We thank thee, God, for eyes to see
The beauty of the earth;
For ears to hear the words of love
And happy sounds of mirth;
For minds that find new thoughts to think,
New wonders to explore;
For health and freedom to enjoy
The good thou hast in store.

Help us remember that to some
The ear and eye and mind
Bring sights and sounds of ugliness,

And only sadness find.
Help us remember that to them
The world has seemed unfair;
That we should strive to bring to them
The beauty all may share.

O may our eyes be open, Lord,
To see our neighbors' need,
And may our ears be kept alert
Their cries of help to heed.
Make keen our minds to plan the best
For one another's good,
That all the world shall be at last
One friendly neighborhood.[4]

OF MANY COLORS

Birds are of many colors,
  On branch, and roof, and wall;
And yet they seem to cherish
  No prejudice at all.
Flowers are many colors,
  Each to the springtime lends
A tint that is distinctive
  And yet they all seem friends.
Rainbows have many colors,
  Yet no malicious stress
Was ever known to blemish
  Their common loveliness.
Only the human species
  Gives or denies its grace
On that particular basis—
  The color of a face.[5]

THINE THE GIFTS WE BRING

Father, we beseech thy blessing
On this gift we offer here.
We who know thy generous bounty,
Help us share it far and near.
Make us ready always, eager,
Quick to answer to thy call:
Thine the giving, ours the living;
Help us serve, thy children all.[6]

WE'D CLASP OUR HANDS

If I knew you and you knew me;
If both of us could clearly see,
And, with an inner light, divine
The meaning of your heart and mine;
I'm sure that we should differ less;
And clasp our hands in friendliness;
Our thoughts would pleasantly agree;
If I knew you and you knew me.[7]

COLOR

The fire was burning brightly. It sent long dancing shadows in among the tall pine trees. It lighted up the tepee not far off. It shone upon the ruddy face of the Indian chief as he bent above the arrows he was feathering. It shone on the face of the boy beside him, his fine eager eyes intent upon his father's busy hands.

"What are you thinking of, my son?" asked the chief, after a long silence.

"Those pale-faces today," the boy answered, slowly. "I did not know, my father, that there were men whose skin was a different color from ours."

The old chief grunted as he laid aside his finished arrow and reached for another. "There are many things, my son, that you will learn as the years go by," he said. "See, now, what colors can you find here in these feathers?"

The boy touched the little heap of feathers with strong, slim fingers. "There are feathers of all colors," he answered, thoughtfully, "just as there are birds of every hue. Here are red, and blue, and white, and yellow."

There was silence for a long moment. Then the old Indian spoke again. "And is it not the same with the flowers?" he asked. "Are there not flowers of all colors in these woods?"

The boy nodded. "And then, there are the rabbits!" he exclaimed, suddenly. "There are brown rabbits, and black rabbits, and white ones! I had never thought of it before."

"As it is with the birds, and with the flowers, and with the rabbits, so it is with men." The chief stared into the fire. "In this land where once were only red men, now are others. There are men with white skins, and men with yellow skins, and some with brown, and some with black. But we are all men. The Great Spirit made us all."

The boy was growing sleepy. He stretched out beside the fire, his head pillowed on his arms. "It would be a strange world if there were not many colors. I should not like it half so well," he murmured.

"All of the ways of the Great Spirit are wise and good, my son." The chief gathered his things together and stood up. He looked from the boy beside the fire to the tall dark pine trees and up to the starry, peaceful sky. "He who planned the glowing colors of the birds and the varied tints of the flowers, planned also the different colored skins of men! His ways are wise and good!" The wind stirred among the pine branches; the fire crackled and sputtered. Far away a night owl hooted. But the Indian boy slept.[8]

GROWING FOOD IS A WORK WITH GOD

Let us look in, as if by television, on some African Christians. As they started out to plant in the spring, they sang gaily and with prayers dedicated their tools, strength, seeds, and time to the God-given task of tilling well the soil.

Rains came. Corn, beans, peanuts, and other plants sprouted and grew. In the humid climate of the coast, people sweated as they carried humus and cultivated to help the soil drink in the dews and nourish the roots. They sang as they toiled.

Harvest! Singing Christians could be seen gathering in their harvest. They were already talking of their Thanksgiving service. How would they give thanks?

The great time has come! At dawn on the appointed Sunday, they gather. Some have bags of corn, beans, peanuts, and other foods. Some have fat chickens. Some have baskets of eggs. Some even have little pigs. Some bring their own handicrafts—pots made of fine clay with loving skill. Their gifts are ready. They leave them under tree or bush and enter the church.

First they worship God and thank Him for life and for the privilege and joy of adding their energies to His great laws and bringing forth abundance of good food and other things. Then, when the singing swells into an exulting anthem of praise and joy, they march, shouldering their gifts and laying them gaily, yet lovingly and reverently, upon the altar.

This is just one little scene. All over the world, groups

of people who believe in God pause at harvest time to marvel at the miracles by which food appears, and to give thanks that now they have food to keep them alive through the winter.

One of the lovely Jewish festivals is the Feast of Booths, a "time of rejoicing." Families sometimes build a little arbor in the yard, with the children helping. Here they eat for a week. It is a little camp shelter, in a way. In cities where families are crowded, some have gardens, or put branches and fruit on an apartment balcony. In the synagogue there is a large booth or "succah"; parties are held in it for the children. The custom goes back many centuries to the time when the ancestors of the Jewish people were protected by God in the wilderness, when they had no homes. Farmers from early times have set up little booths in their fields and vineyards to take care of the ripening fruits of the harvest. Through this custom, the Jewish people remind themselves each year anew of God's goodness and faithfulness to them: "Seed time and harvest never fail." [9]

(*Note:* If in a long-term summer camp some simple items of food have been grown in a garden plot by the campers, a "Thanksgiving" service may be held by them. If the group is interfaith, the service might include certain ideas the Jewish children will remember from their own families' observances, as well as the general expression of thankfulness. If the camp is large, the First Thanksgiving in America may be dramatized, with some playing the part of Indians bringing their gifts, too. Thus is symbolized the dependence of all peoples upon God, the Giver; and our common responsibility to till the soil carefully and well, and to work against erosion and all other tendencies to plunder and pillage the planet. We show our thankfulness by the way we use God's gifts.)

WE THANK YOU, GOD, FOR THE FOOD WE EAT

We thank You, God, for the food we eat,
For good fresh vegetables, fruits and meat.

For pure sweet milk and fresh white bread,
For all the foods by which we're fed,

For farmers who work in dairies and fields,
For all the riches the good earth yields,

For trainmen and truckmen who carry it far
Bring it to us right where we are,

For grocers and milkmen who come to our door,
For bakers and butchers who work in the store.

Help us with others Your bounty to share
So all in the world may know Your loving care.[10]

THE DRUM THAT SAID THANK YOU

Little Grey Owl had wanted a drum for a long time. He would soon be seven years old and he surely could learn to play a drum. Every time he asked his father to make him one he would answer, "maybe so—sometime."

It was just one more moon until the harvest festival and at that time all the drums in the village would be used for the games and songs. Grey Owl thought to beat a drum at the festival would be the finest thing that could happen.

That night his father came home with a part of a tree trunk. Grey Owl wondered about it. Could it be that his father was going to make a drum? Sure enough, his father began to cut out the inside of it and he said, "Do you know of an Indian boy around here who could learn to play a drum before the festival?" Grey Owl smiled a big smile.

"I know a boy who would try very hard. His name is Grey Owl. He has a very good kind father."

All the rest of the day his father worked on the drum and the next morning Grey Owl helped him stretch a skin across it. He could hardly wait until his father fixed the stick he was to use in beating his drum. He struck the skin with his hand. "Thud, thud," said the drum. Oh, how fine it would be when he could really play on it!

Soon the stick was ready and he beat on his drum. "Tum, tum, tum, tum, tum."

A big smile spread all over his face and he said, "Listen to this, my father, the drum says 'Thank you,' " and he beat a "Tum tum" which sounded first like the Indian word for "thank you."

The boys who beat the drums at the harvest festival games were very happy, but the happiest one was Grey Owl.[11]

WHO IS MY BROTHER?

Who is my brother?
Only the son of my mother?
Shall I forget that other—
The stranger in need,
The hurt child who doth bleed,
Fellow creature whose creed
Differs from mine?
Father, is he not thine?
If he is thine,
Then no difference I see,

Because I know
He is brother to me.[12]

ON THE WINGS OF IMAGINATION

On the wings of imagination
may I ride
into the lives of others,
and live at their side.
Forgetting myself
and the life I live,
entering another's life,
to live as he lives.
If I were *he,*
and this happened to *me,*
From him no different
would I be.
I would do as he does,
no different would I be.
May I step out of my own life,
on the wings of imagination,
and have the joy
and the rich experience
of living with others.[13]

I WILL BRING PEACE

I will bring peace and love and silence.
There is no way to bring peace
unless I can be that peace.
There is no way to give love
unless I can be that love.
There is no way to bring silence
unless I can be that silence.[14]

WHO IS MY NEIGHBOR?

The family next door,
Or just across the street?
The chance person I meet?
Yes, but even more
The stranger unknown.
Are his needs not my own?—
The child who lives in a tent,
Old man whose back is bent,
Ragged boy of the slums
Who lives on snatches and crumbs,
The woman in the field,
Factory worker whose yield
Brings comfort to me?
All people—
No matter who they be—
Are neighbor to me.[15]

IF ALL PEOPLE ONLY KNEW—

If it were taught in all schools that there are more than 200,000,000 homeless in the world today, more than 1,000,000,000 human beings simply hungry, that half the world's population cannot read, then I am certain that mankind would feel so united in one common striving for welfare that it would be very hard to raise nation against nation.[16]

WORK

Let us be willing
In all our work—
Mowing, mending, cleaning house,
Our duty never shirk.

Earnest, careful, cheerful,
Let us do our part.
When we're kind and busy,
There's joy within the heart.

Let us be helpful
All through the day—
Sharing, giving, bringing joy
To all who pass our way.
We'll clasp hands in friendship,
Fold our hands to pray,
Ask that God's near presence
Be with us on life's way.

Let us remember
All those who work
Sowing, planting, reaping grain
And growing food to eat.
Buying, selling, serving
All the needs of man,
Working hard and striving
To carry out God's plan.[17]

CARE

A doctor visited his patients,
Giving to each one the treatment he needed to make him well,
And God was pleased with the doctor's work.

A teacher helped a boy to learn to read,
And the books which he read helped him to know more about the world in which he lived,
And God was pleased with the teacher's work.

A school guard watched the traffic
And helped the school children across the street in safety
And God was pleased with the school guard's work.

A missionary went to India
And taught the people
  That God is their loving Father
  And they were his children.
And God was pleased with the missionary's work.

A minister helped his people
To find Christian ways of living together in God's world,
And God was pleased with the minister's work.[18]

7

Prayers

O GOD, how glad we are that You thought of giving us many kinds of weather, and not just one kind. We know that sometimes it must be cloudy, for the farms to have rain and for the flowers and trees to grow. We love the different seasons. Help us to enjoy them even more as we think of Your plan in making our world. Whatever the weather we may be having, may we remember that You are with us and love us. Amen.[1]

Our Father, how beautiful Your thoughts of a world must have been, before You made trees . . . and put songs in birds' throats . . . and gave a gurgling merry murmur to brooks and streams! Thank You for sharing all this beauty with us. Thank You for so much beauty all around the earth everywhere—beauty we have not seen, but can imagine from what we *have* seen. You meant us to enjoy it all very much, didn't You? May we lift up our own thoughts from dwelling on ugly things, and revel in Your beautiful, wonderful world that somehow it may help us be as fine in our lives as Your thought of us must be! Amen.[2]

Father God, right now—this still, holy now when we feel close to You—we want to thank You for all quietness, everywhere. It's fun to have noise, to hear music, to talk back and forth, to sing. But sometimes we like it all hushed and quiet. Thank You for snow, and the softness of it that stills even the tiny rabbit's footfall. Thank You for late starlight and the still shine coming from some distant star so far, right into our very hearts. Thank You for friends to be buddies with, who understand what we mean when we *don't* speak. Thank You for the rests in music, the pauses between the notes that rest our ears and help us hear the melody. Thank You for rest from work and for deep peaceful sleep. We want to pray now that somehow You and we working together may cause all the ugly noises over the world to hush—people quarreling, discords, wrecks, explosions, wars. May we all turn back to You, where all lovely quiet comes from. Amen.[3]

PART THREE

WITH JUNIORS AND YOUNG TEENS

8

Worship Ways with Juniors and Young Teens

THE TWO WORDS "security" and "adventure" are keys to the guidance of pre-adolescent and adolescent boys and girls, in camp or anywhere. In fact, one can scarcely begin to understand them—or to help them understand themselves—unless one is aware of these two big drives pulling them at the same time.

During childhood they could scarcely wait to reach ten, and then their teens. But now, strange, bewildering sensations come with physical maturing. Muscles do not always do what the mind tells them to. Sometimes life seems to be so terrifically full of fun and of new things to do and be, that one rushes to the top of the hill and stretches one's arms wide to the glorious world and sea and sky. And one makes up secret words with one's contemporaries, words that others would not understand and that convey to those who know this very special feeling of being a young teen. But at other times life does not go so well. *Everything* goes horribly wrong. One wanders off where no adults will ask what is the matter, and dreams movie-like scenes where one is the misunderstood heroine or hero, and where at last the world bows at one's feet.

The mind is sharp and keen during these years. In fact, it is said that a person does his most honest thinking in early adolescence. One must puzzle out many a strange problem, both personal and world, but particularly about one's family. All sorts of unimagined abilities are there for the trying. Athletic skill is considered the acme, and athletes are crowned as heroes.

The young teen is thus trying to get his self-picture in focus, to know for sure what manner of person he is. Often that picture is blurred. Others fail to treat him as if he were as grown-up as he knows he is. But sometimes too much is expected, and he fails miserably. Then the self-image shrivels. He is reaching constantly, sometimes almost desperately, for sureness as to what he can do. Meanwhile, he is cutting himself away from apron strings and demanding a chance to decide for himself how late he will stay out at night, what clothes to buy, and what popular music.

Here are evidences of the dramatic "force field" going on within young teens, of the pull toward certain basic securities together with the stronger pull of new adventure. Physically, there must be the security of food and, sometimes (although this is steadfastly fought), sleep. Fatigue comes quickly. Hence the characteristic adolescent flop, on whatever is handy and in whatever position one lands. Yet ever there is the surging onward, the trying of new skills, the rushing toward new experiences.

In no area of young teens' lives is this dramatic interplay more powerful than in their social reachings. In moving a step outward from family dependence, they must find "social security" in those of their own age. Hence the queer "cults," the language, the identical dress, the rage over popular singers, the interminable telephone calls. Girls, having developed more rapidly than boys, look toward the group of fellows just older. Sometimes the too-early "going steady," and emotional involvements that wreck young lives, begins simply from this urge to have a buddy one can depend on to take one places. Sometimes the adventurous pull of the new, without counterbalancing securities in convictions and ideals, leads over the brink in sex experiences. Or gangs may turn thief or vandal, more for the thrill of something new to do than from a desire for goods or from evil intent, for some of the juvenile delinquents are from well-to-do homes.

Emotions are tender and volatile. Colors are felt poignantly. Beauty is painfully real, and so are hurt and ugliness. Religiously, the young teen years are strangely significant: midway between childhood and adulthood, at life's crossroads. Among primitive peoples these are years for initiation into tribal secrets through unforgettably impressive ceremonials. Among more cultivated people, these are years for joining the church, or for being brought into the fellowship of the adults of one's worshiping group. Such rites, rich with tradition and heavy with significance, do help the adolescent bring his self-picture into clear focus. Now at last he knows what manner of person to think himself. He is *accepted.* Organizations and clubs for young people in the teen years do well to have investiture services of beauty and meaning. Camp traditions likewise enhance the self-picture and the sureness of belonging.

But for young teens otherwise secure in all areas of their lives, there is still a pervading restlessness, a wistfulness, a feeling that there *must* be a God somewhere, that they must find and establish their relationship with

Him. With all the eager adventurousness of their young spirits, they *reach*. A lovely nature hymn, with the beauty of God's world around, may suddenly open the door. And now they feel and know. Or perhaps that moment comes when one is worried and hurt and tries to pray—and discovers somehow that one is understood by One who knows. Particularly thrilling is the awareness that sometimes comes early, sometimes later, that one's own life is a part of God's plan; that it makes a difference to His purposes and to the world what one decides to do with one's life.

Worship from the Inside Out

Therefore, worship at camp or anywhere with young teens should be sincere, from the inside, or not at all. It is entirely too easy for counselors, and young leaders themselves, to wrest a certain false security from "putting on programs" neatly and nicely, doing all the parts well. Some whose egos are sick for attention may even win praise from adult leaders for the way they pray aloud or speak in services. But this is dangerous ground. During the young teen years, habits of sincerity or insincerity are easily forged.

Camp brooks nothing insincere or artificial in any aspect of its life, certainly not in prayer or worship observances. Stress should not be put upon formal programs and upon getting boys and girls to participate; rather stress should at all times be upon being honest with one's self and with God and with one another. Any expression—singing, praying, speaking, silence—would simply be a matter of sharing what was first felt in the heart.

Counselors of young teens need to be sensitively attuned both to God and to the youngsters; alert and flexible to the possibilities in the passing moment; yet tactful enough not to urge or to say too much or speak too soon. The "consciousness of God in the daily routine" is the first essential. When this is there, little need be done in the way of providing formal set services; the content of any special services may grow gradually out of various earlier experiences in the camp community. The way young teens plan for their morning quiet time or angelus or other services should grow from their needs. The pattern again comes *from the inside*—from what they are wondering (adventure), and from what they are discovering (security).

The important thing is not to get a service planned, but that their worship be real to them now, at their stage of growing. They can evolve their own meaningful camp customs.

Should There Be Planned Services for Young Teens?

This is being written with a widely divergent variety of situations in mind. No blanket answer can be made. If it is planned so as to fit into camp life (not just into the schedule), an occasional service can enhance the camp experience, in fact it can be one of its high points. Often returning campers tell first about "morning quiet time" or "angelus" or "day's end." Too, when there is a regular worship observance, there will be more natural, spontaneous responses on hikes and in other phases of the camp day.

At two major times, many camps tend to have planned services: morning and vespers. Some have "all-alone meditation" before breakfast, first putting into campers' hands some brief devotional aids. Some have "thought for the day" in the cabin or shelter group. In some camps a leader gives a brief thought at the breakfast table, after the meal has been eaten and the tables cleared.

Sunset time seems especially fitting for a service. A "silent trail" leading to the hilltop for vespers can be a holy time; a choir lined on either side of the trail may sing a "prelude." "Nobody speaks on silent trail and at vespers but God and Mrs. Gilmore," remarked a camper.

Ceremonials for beginning camp have been previously mentioned. There would also be ceremonials for closing camp. Birthday observances increase adolescents' sense of belonging. One camp makes a ritual out of a tree-planting each year. There may be an Indian council ring (with discussion and stories of brotherhood leading to thoughts of world peace, even though a "pipe" is not smoked). There may be a festival of the nations with games and songs, and maybe even food of other lands, and a gay array of colorful costumes. There may be a lantern-hike to the music of an accordion or guitar, and a moonlight boat ride afterward. There may be a Hebrew nomad campfire with all in costume and with the story-teller recounting age-old lore of the patriarchs, and a choir chanting antiphonal psalms.

How Should We Plan with Young Teens?

Committees of boys and girls may discuss first with their counselor the meaning of worship, how it should be always sincere and "from the inside," how there should never be a hymn sung or Scripture or other material read or prayer spoken that is not sincerely felt. This is a part of "good sportsmanship with God." Then they may consider the particular need for the immediate service. What will the campers be thinking about as they come to the service? What would help them feel God near? What would help them think with Him in prayer?

Thus they begin—not wrong-end-to as many youths do who turn to a theme and dig out poems and selections on the subject, but with the thought of their personal relationship with God—and plan straightforwardly from there. The experience of helping to plan is in itself meaningful, if campers are guided by a thoughtful counselor to plan with sincerity.

Nor must the focus be upon themselves as they take part. Sometimes adolescents, starved for recognition, like the role of performer in worship services. But as each one is asked to take part, the idea of feeling what he is doing and making it sincere should be discussed with him. He should see how the service may help the group draw nearer to God, then see his part in that light. Planners and participants should not be concerned to have others say, "We enjoyed it," or "That was smooth," or "Well planned." Rather, they pray that through what is said and done, or through the silence, someone may come into closer fellowship with God. Thus for planners and all others who are to take part, there is first a prayerful spirit.

Usually, a service has a theme that helps tie together the varied parts. The theme should not be chosen from a book. Nor should it be adapted from some story or poem somebody likes and wants to plan around. Rather, the theme should grow out of the immediate needs of the group. What problems or needs are uppermost in their thoughts? What would they wish to pray about? Not all services need a subject or theme. Actually, the theme of all real worship is that of seeking God, focusing Godward. That should be theme enough.

There is no set order in which materials should be put together in a service. One service may be brief, almost entirely a thanksgiving to God. Another may be a time of intercessory prayer. Usually, the outward order will grow out of the inward feeling.

First, we seek to center our thoughts upon God, to focus wandering attention, to let minds come to rest in greater awareness of Him, to let His Spirit speak to us, to still our inmost selves to listen. During a prelude played, perhaps, on a violin or maybe during the humming of a hymn, we may all take this first step together. Somehow, when we do, we feel drawn closer to one another as well as to God. The Spirit of God *does* draw us into a fellowship.

We may wish to express our joy at this experience by singing a hymn of praise; or perhaps by a verse from a psalm, or by a poem lifting our thoughts to the Maker of the beauty of the earth.

Next, we are ready to look at ourselves and others, with God's help, more lovingly. We may examine some problem we face, or some choice we need to make. We may pray together about it. We may seek forgiveness for wrongs done others, and wrongs inflicted upon our own personalities. We may think of our use, or misuse, of time and money; of our health; of our earth—and ask God's guidance in being better users of what He has given. Sometimes a story helps us think through such things; sometimes a drama; sometimes a few brief suggestions and then silence so that each may think his own deeper thoughts; sometimes a discussion or role-playing that pictures choices; sometimes a film will set before us a new challenge.

The third step is that of making answer. After the challenge, campers may want to be silent a little while;

or a hymn of dedication may rightly express what is most felt. Or there may be a fellowship of prayer or some other closing.

Plans should be simple and right to the point. Let there be just one central basic idea and not too much material brought in. If there is music, let it not be announced as "special"; rather suggest, "May we continue to meditate as the music gives us its message."

Many planners tend to use too much material. Even though this book contains materials, we repeat: *do not* use any more than you must at any one time! First, seek to be led by the Spirit of One Higher; then try to express, however haltingly, what is being felt in the group. Never let a read prayer cut off someone from praying, even silently, his own prayer in his heart. Always encourage campers to make their own expressions of praise, of thinking with God about their lives, of dedication. Some may write—let them create their own poems that call to worship or express new ideas. Let them write prayers if they fear to start one aloud by themselves. Some may prepare to tell stories, or work out dramatic episodes showing vividly what concerns them most.

No service should be built around materials. Most groups use too much; have too many words, too little silence. Only that which touches off a living spark in the thoughts of the planners should be chosen; for, in turn, it may touch off a spark in the others. Inspired writings are like imprisoned light from out other burning hearts that have experienced the vital quality of fellowship with God we all are seeking.

Yet a selection (such as one from this book), no matter how alive and inspired it appeared to writer, compiler, and planners, may be killed by deadly dull reading. If a camper is to take a part in a service, let him first catch this living fire, feeling the meaning and the glow of the selection. Then let him practice with utmost care, making sure that any unfamiliar words are explained to him and that he pronounces them correctly. He becomes ready to transmit the message through his own voice, so that in turn others may grasp the meaning. Those who are getting ready to take part in a service or ceremonial may wish to meet a half hour early for some quiet time together and perhaps a prayer. For they want what they say and do to ring true.

The other half of the planning experience is thinking through the service with the counselor after it is over. The first questions would be: "Were we sincere?" "Were we putting God first and not ourselves?" Then, "How might we have planned or participated better?" Failures as well as successes can teach if the reasons for the failures are analyzed honestly. Boys and girls come to take their responsibilities for participating in worship more seriously when they know they will evaluate afterward.

Aids and Reminders

Music, in all its myriad forms, is of course the most potent aid for worship and an aid for good fellowship in camp as well. If the camp is a singing camp, the chances are that there will be a quick readiness for worship as well.

The best leadership for camp music with young teens is an able counselor who loves the beautiful but can start where the campers are in teaching them to know and love it, too. If the music counselor can first catch the wave length of the campers and then gradually help them learn a number of good folk and fellowship songs, he can help them learn hymns and even spiritual classics with joy.

Sometimes young teen campers are already conditioned to cheap, tawdry, crude stuff, both in the fellowship and fun singing and in spiritual songs. The leader's approach would not be overtly negative, but he would see to it that no opportunity was given for starting the cheaper songs (no other counselor should start songs, either); by teaching new and lovelier ones daily and letting the campers hear and feel the beauty, gradually a taste for the better music will be built.

Those working with worship-planning committees should co-operate closely with the music counselor, so that hymns and songs can be taught a goodly time ahead of the need to use them in a service. If possible, some lovely mental pictures should be built along with the singing. If a nature hymn is being taught, the campers might relate certain scenes around the camp to the various stanzas. Thus the singing in the worship service can be "from the inside."

Never—neither with young teens nor with any other age—should pious words be put to popular tunes. If the singing is for fun, let it be honestly so. If the singing is for worship, let it be honestly so. The practice of "clowning" spirituals should be stopped sternly. Many of the spirituals arose out of deep aspiration, even suffering. Some are now finding their way into the best church hymnals. For example, "Do, Lord . . . do remember me" is a prayer; clowning it by adding "Oh Lordy" (veritable blasphemy, is this not?) between jingly beats and making up silly verses are *not* to be tolerated. "Oh, but when they ask for things we have to let them have what they want," excuses a counselor who is sadly misinterpreting the exercise of the democratic method with young teens.

No camp should have a *laissez-faire* policy. Counselors are there to guide, to lift standards higher, to appeal to that native adventure in young teens for "onward, upward."

Nature hymns will be used most often with young teens in camp. Fortunately, the finest hymns are found in many denominational and other hymnals. Every hymnal is a league of the nations and of the peoples of the earth, as well as a bridge between the centuries. Only the worthy hymns should be used. How can they be distinguished? A "cheap" song that does not belong in worship (no matter how the campers love it) is one dealing with self-centered states of feeling or one appealing more to the feet than to the heart. Songs beginning "I feel so-and-so" do not belong in worship. Real hymns are addressed to God as prayers, or are about Him. Even a hymn telling how sweet is the hour for prayer merely suggests that we pray; it is not God-centered, and it is not a prayer. The better hymns of the modern day affirm the greatness and love of God, and express the challenge that we love and serve our brothers. Spiritual health is built through such aids, as is physical health through good food and sunshine. Such hymns stretch our souls. They give us reach.

How should we teach a hymn for use in worship? Campers should first be allowed to listen to it all through. They might tell what thoughts the music helps them think. They may then read and discuss the words together. Thus they get the "feel" of it. Then they hear and hum and think the words. Soon they can sing it. Always, each time, they go clear through the hymn, not chopping it up for drill.

Some of the fellowship songbooks for camp and outdoor use offer a careful selection of hymns for worship.

Here are some of the newer hymns, more appropriate for young teens than many in the older church hymnals. The vesper hymn, "At Worship," was written by a seventeen-year-old in her first camp. "Youth's Hymn of a New World" gives stirring challenge, as set to Haydn's theme. If only enough youth could know and sing it, it might prove as expressive of the mood of today as was "A Mighty Fortress" in its first usage. A hymn such as "A Mighty Fortress" is timeless, as contemporary now as when it was originally written.

Brief responses to be sung prayerfully may be learned by all or by a camp choir. Campers themselves can compose fitting tunes as well as write words to brief responses. Spirituals sung in reverent spirit are the best beginning and closing for campfire fellowship.

In addition to vocal music, there may be records of music appropriate for instilling reverence or guiding meditation. In some camps, the signals for rising and for lights out are appropriate hymns. Wilderness camps, of course, frown on loudspeaker systems; but there is more to be said for having thoughts of security in God's love suggested to one's mind and heart rather than the raucous rousements of military bugles.

What about aids for the eye as well as for the ear? Nature itself provides the setting in camping. Few indeed are the camps that have not some special spot of beauty to which campers love to repair, and which they will remember all their lives. Little outdoor spots may be arranged by the campers. Sometimes there is a tree-board on which individuals may tack poems or other original contributions from day to day. Some camps have chapels in the woods or green cathedrals. Nothing artificial should be introduced in the camp site, however; it may be that efforts to copy church architecture do not belong in the groves, which were the first temples, anyway. Sometimes a little clearing and seats are all that are needed. No artificial settings should be fabricated. But sometimes campers make candle holders, offering plates, or other symbols of fitting rustic materials; and the very making and dedication become an act of worship.

What about pictures and films? All of life about camp is a picture. But sometimes pictures help along worship or learning experiences. Some nature films introduce the campers to other aspects of nature a far distance from the camp, or demonstrate the mysterious and beautiful balance of nature. If a film is to be used, a conversation should prepare the group for the viewing; and there would be appropriate follow-through.

Stories have a wide variety of uses in young teen camps, for worship as well as for other purposes. When a story is to be used in a worship service, it is approached in a particular way. Many details may be omitted, and the central message allowed to shine through without moralizing one whit. It is told simply, quietly, with campers drawing their own conclusions. Perhaps a prayer would follow, or simply silence for thinking.

Closely akin to stories are the various dramatic ways of living the plots, acting them out. Campers can take a plot from everyday life, ad-libbing the roles of the characters they have taken. With young teens, problems of daily relationships back home can be brought into the open. At one camp, some problems in the camp itself were role-played, and solutions worked out happily through discussion. In this is release, both for those who are acting and for the whole group who participate vicariously. Only in camps set up for therapy, with trained personnel on the staff, should anything as serious as psychodrama be attempted. Yet to an extent, all good drama is psychodrama in that it helps persons see life more clearly, bring feelings into the open, find ways of resolving problems. Young teens love to make and use shadow puppets or paper-bag puppets or marionettes.

Choral reading, too, is a dramatic medium. With a prepared poem or reading or Scripture, charted as to voices of "dark" or "light" or "medium" timbre, the choir rehearses until unison is felt. If choral reading is to get a message across, it must come *from the inside.* Sometimes group reading is done by the whole group (say, of a Bible narrative, with the whole group reading the description and individual characters taking the solo parts).

Young teens can make many of their own worship aids. Take, for example, a litany. Far more meaningful than choosing one from a book would be the experience of talking over together some reminders of God's love they have noted that very day. A secretary jots down each spontaneous comment. Easily, then, these are arranged with a refrain decided upon by the group. In this way, some learn first to pray aloud.

Longer ceremonials can be worked out by young teens also, and they love to plan. Most camps have traditional services or ceremonials, and the anticipation reaches a white heat as the time draws near. We have mentioned earlier ceremonials for beginning and closing camp. Sometimes Indian lore is woven into the campfire rituals, especially on an evening when Big Chief Such-and-So comes suddenly into the fire circle. Ceremonials can be built around the moon, or the water, or the hills, or the trees. In many church camps, a closing service of fagot burning (each camper tossing a twig on the fire to symbolize some practice he wants to have burned out of his life) is traditional. In others, candlelight is used. Always when lights are low and the stars are overhead, the magic curtain of illusion falls and imagination kindles. Such are life's luminous moments. Who knows what young teen sitting by the fire some night as a story is told, resolves that some day he, too . . . with God's help?

And so, all we can do in the worship guidance of young teens is to help them find new security in a firmer foundation of knowledge of God's love and creation and of their part in His plan, and joyous fellowship with Him through worship and prayer; and at the same time, to help them feel ever the tug of the unexplored, the call to ever higher adventures.

9

Finding God More Fully through His Handiwork

GOD IS HERE

At dusk there comes a call to rest and pray
From misted hill, from stream and woodland near,
God speaks. His voice is in the wood-bird's throat,
And maples, willows whisper, "God is here."
"God's here!"—we hear it echoed in the breeze—
"God's here!"—a quiet peace broods o'er our fire;
Soon now the stars appearing one by one
Find mirrored here, true hearts that never tire.[1]

WORSHIP

Silvery mists, moonlit glow
Winds, and the rippling stream,
Fields of grain, showers of rain,
All speak of God to me.

Fires and the sunset evening glow
Blossoms that flower—winds that blow
Tell me His care is sure—
  Worship silently,
  Worship prayerfully—God.[2]

WHEN WE PRAY

Bible reading: Jesus teaches His disciples to pray, Luke 11:1-4.

Do you talk with God as to your Father? Do you believe that God more than anyone else is interested in what you do? God wants you to want to talk with Him. He wants to help you. But He does not do it unless you give Him a chance.

Will you pray to God now?

First, will you thank Him for something that has made you happy?

Then, will you ask Him to guide you in your actions today that you may follow Jesus?

And will you ask Him for the strength and the courage to live as He should like you to?

Now, will you sit still for a minute to think about God, your Father?

> I have a watch to keep,
> And if I fail,
> If I let work or sleep
> Or care prevail,
> And do not pause to pray to God at dawn,
> When at the close of day I sit and yawn,
> Not only body then, but soul is tired,
> Because my day has not been
> God-inspired! [3]

CONVERSATION

God, who art in heaven, I like to talk to You.
Most people call it praying, but it's talking that I do.
I talk when I'm in trouble; I tell You when I'm glad;

For though You don't need telling, it helps me when I'm sad.
And you are always listening, for You never turn away,
And when I need an answer, You know just what to say.
Your voice is very quiet, but I know it can be found.
I hear it like a whisper; I feel it like a sound.[4]

OUR CAMP WORLD AT DAWN

O how lovely is the dawning
As its colors brightly blend,
O how gorgeous is the sunset
When it brings day's perfect end.
O how lovely is the evening
With its shadows and its breeze.
O how lovely is the night time
Making whispers through the trees.
O how lovely is the starlight
Shining down from up above.
O how perfect is this world of ours
Because it comes from God's own love.[5]

HIS WONDERS NEVER CEASE

This is my Father's world,
And all his people must
Live lives of love and service too
And in him put our trust.
This is my Father's world.
And we are full of peace
Because we find him kind and true
His wonders never cease.[6]

HIS LOVING PLAN FULFILL

This is my Father's world,
Let campers upright be,

In all we say and all we do
We strive to follow thee.
This is my Father's world,
I'll try to do his will
And help all people everywhere
His loving plan fulfill.[7]

INDIAN UNDERSTANDING OF THE TWENTY-THIRD PSALM

The Great Father above is a Shepherd Chief. I am His, and with Him I want not.

He throws out to me a rope and the name of the rope is Love, and He draws me to where the grass is green and the water is not dangerous, and I eat and lie down satisfied.

Sometimes my heart is very weak and falls down, but He lifts it up again and draws me into a good road. His name is Wonderful.

Sometime, it may be very soon, it may be longer, it may be a long, long time, He will draw me into a place between mountains. It is dark there but I'll not draw back. I'll not be afraid, for it is there between the mountains that the Shepherd Chief will meet me, and the hunger I have felt in my heart all through this life will be satisfied.

Sometimes He makes the love rope into a whip, but afterwards He gives me a staff to lean on.

He spreads a table before me with all kinds of food. He puts His hand upon my head and all the tired is gone. My cup He fills till it runs over.

What I tell you is true, I lie not. These roads that are away ahead will stay with me through this life, and afterward I will go to live in the Big Tepee and sit down with the Shepherd Chief forever.[8]

UNDERSTANDING SOME OF NATURE'S STRANGENESS

Campers may enjoy playing with some magical tricks that are really scientific experiments of a sort. They will think how strange these seem, yet they work by law. Groups may do such things as—

1. Make a musical scale out of bottles filled with different amounts of water.
2. See how many pennies can be dropped into a glass brimful of water.
3. Electrify a piece of woolen material so that it will attract metal objects.

Properly speaking, man never invents anything. He merely discovers an invention of God's. In our world of science we should begin to help these boys and girls understand that science is reponsible for the results of its work. They may be interested to know that many prominent scientists declined the invitation to work on the atomic bomb. To discover new natural laws is a useful and splendid thing, but to use them so that they help rather than hurt humanity is the obligation of one who knows nature's God.

God does not use only the laws of nature to help him with his world; he uses men, too. Sometime ago some men went out to that part of our country where the loosened soil had blown away in terrible dust storms. They worked according to the laws of science that they knew. Some day the soil will be entirely restored, grass will grow and homes will be built again. . . . More than ten years ago a young man went out to what was then desert country. He said he was going to raise oranges. Everyone laughed. But he is raising oranges. The desert has disappeared. Flowers and fruits are everywhere.

Men made a great and mighty dam and water flows through irrigation ditches into the desert.[9]

ANTIPHONAL

Leader: O give thanks unto the Lord for the tall, majestic mountains all covered with trees, towering upward to God.

Group: Praise ye the Lord for the high mountains and rippling lake.

Leader: O give thanks unto the Lord for the trees.

Group: Praise ye the Lord for the tulip poplar trees,
Praise ye the Lord for the towering pines.
Praise ye the Lord for the quaking aspens.

Leader: O give thanks unto the Lord for the earth and water.

Group: Praise ye the Lord for the clear springs and lakes.
Praise ye the Lord for the cool mountain springs.
Praise ye the Lord for the bubbling springs.

Leader: O give thanks unto the Lord for the earth and everything in it.

Group: Praise ye the Lord for the birds.
Praise ye the Lord for the glorious scenery.
Praise ye the Lord for the beauty of the earth.

All: Praise ye the Lord for the majestic mountains,
For the towering pine,
For the rippling lake.
Praise ye the Lord for everything that moves and breathes.[10]

SALUTE TO THE TREES

Many a tree is found in the wood
And every tree for its use is good:

Some for the strength of the gnarled root,
Some for the sweetness of flower or fruit,
Some for the shelter against the storm,
And some to keep the hearth-stone warm;
Some for the roof and some for the beam,
And some for a boat to breast the stream—
In the wealth of the wood since the world began
The trees have offered their gifts to man.

But the glory of trees is more than their gifts;
'Tis a beautiful wonder of life that lifts,
From a wrinkled seed in an earth-bound clod,
A column, an arch in the temple of God,
A pillar of power, a dome of delight,
A shrine of song, and a joy of sight!
Their roots are the nurses of rivers in birth;
Their leaves are alive with the breath of the earth;
They shelter the dwellings of man; and they bend
O'er his grave with the look of a loving friend.[11]

THE SUMMIT

A sparrow idles over me,
Looking for the sun. I see
The breathless crags upon the edge
Of hill.
        The darkened lodge
Is soon below. The luring call
To see the bended bush and all
The proud and patient rocks are there
On top—in deep, soul-stirring air.
The haughty summit now is mine.
Beyond the leaves I see a line
Of twilight where the faded day
In rugged silence gives its gray

Farewell. A solitary tree
Is paused, and praying reverently.[12]

WHEN TREES TALK

The talking oak
To the ancients spoke.
But any tree
Will talk to me.

What truths I know
I garnered so,
But those who want to talk and tell
And those who will not listeners be
Will never hear a syllable
From out the lips of any tree.[13]

TO A PINE GROVE IN WINTER

Pine trees, against a cold white sky,
I sing of your courage,
I sing of your monarchy on the hillside;
Your velvet darkness,
The sound of music like a swift river
That issues from your branches when the wind is high;
Of the celestial air that you exhale,
And of the frankincense of your evergreen needles;
You are like old warriors of mighty valor
Who keep staunch vigil when the rest have fled.
Lofty pines, I salute you! You have taught me that patience
Is part of life's plan, and conquers all else.[14]

STRENGTH AND BEAUTY IN THE TREES

Summer time is a time of trees. In the spring trees are a mass of glorious bloom, and in the fall trees are a riot of color. But in the summer time trees are doing the work for which they are intended, the work of producing fruit, the work of bringing to maturity the product by which men and animals are fed, the work of supplying seeds by which trees are perpetuated through the centuries.

The oldest living things on earth are trees. In the giant Sequoia and Mariposa groves of California we have living organisms which were fullgrown when Jesus and his disciples walked the face of the earth, and which had their beginning when much of human history was still hidden in the fog of obscurity.

Some of the world's strongest power is wrapped up in a tree. A little seedling blown across a lake will take root in a bit of moss hidden in the crevice of a flat rock. With the passing of years as the seedling grows it seeks deeper rootage and greater nourishment. Day by day it sends its tiny roots deeper into the scarcely perceivable apertures in the rock. Day by day it grows a little higher gaining strength to send its roots a little deeper. Day by day the rock is slowly but steadily pushed asunder until the time comes, after many years, when the tree breaks the rock with its quiet but surging power. And the rock which was once its greatest hindrance to growth becomes its anchor and stay in storm and strife.

A tree is a source of comfort and an object of beauty. It combines utility with art. In its branches birds make nests. In its shade animals rest from the heat of noon day. Its fruit gives food for hungry men. At the same time the upward reach of its branches toward the sky, the horizon, the radiance of its springtime green, the intensity of its autumn crimson and gold, make a tree an object of beauty seldom equalled in God's world. All the world agrees when a poet says, "Poems are made by fools like me, but only God can make a tree." [15]

A CAMPER GROWS AWARE

I walked into the woods one day,
The trees were oh so tall,
That's why I guess I felt akin
To everything that's small.

The air was soft and sweet with spring,
The moss was oh so green,
Vine-patterned like a casket,
And fit for any queen.

The noise on streets was far away,
Here was a different stir;
Leaf move, bee hum, small creature pause,
And then a bird would whirr.

I held my breath from sheer delight,
Then slipt by ash and fern
Back to the dusty road again
And more dull things to learn.

The world looked just the same outside,
Things are just what they seem.
Inside I knew 'twas different
Because I'd lived a dream.[16]

LIKE A TREE AGAINST THE SKY

Let me stand upon the hilltop
  Like a tree against the sky.
Let me mark the way for travelers—
  Rooted deep, and pointing high.

Here surveyors chart their courses,
  Climbers, lost, regain the trail,
Kneel, with new and clearer vision
  Of the long-sought Holy Grail.

Keep me pure O Breath of God,
Worthy of this crest so high!
Help me stand upon the hilltop
Like a tree against the sky.[17]

WE PRAY THEE, OUR FATHER

Help us to be straight and tall like the trees
And happy like the birds that sing so sweetly,
We pray thee, Our Father.
Help us to be lovely like the flowers and grass
And swift like the rushing stream,
We pray thee, Our Father.
Help us to be strong like the towering rocks
And busy like the honey bees
We pray thee, Our Father.
Help us to give cheer like the beautiful sun
And be silent like the heavens above
We pray thee, Our Father.
Help us to appreciate all thy beautiful creation
And to love thee more each day.
We pray thee, in thy name, Our Father. Amen.[18]

MY PLACE IN THE SUN

My Father has need of the birds and the flowers,
And a place for each beautiful tree;
And so I am sure in his wonderful plan
There's a place and a mission for me.

So wherever I go, and in all that I do,
I crave the clear vision to see
My place in my Father's own wonderful plan,
My task and his blessing for me.[19]

CEREMONIAL OF PLANTING A TREE

One of the traditions of a camp in western North Carolina is a tree-planting service when a white pine is planted to beautify camp, to hold banks from eroding, and to give campers the glow of satisfaction from carrying out a significant project as a result of their camp discussions. A counselor wrote the following poem to be used at this service:

In the beginning, God said, . . .
Let the earth with trees be spread,
And it was even so;
And then God said, 'tis good—now grow.

And since that day all trees have grown
Up toward their maker;—praises shown
By lifting up their arms each morn
To greet with joy, the day newborn.

This is our prayer; may it be so,
That, as we plant this tree, we show
Our part in Thy creative plan,
When Thou didst cause the trees to stand.

Impart Thy blessings on this tree,
That it may grow, and ever be,
A symbol of our hopes which rise,
To Thee who made the earth and skies.[20]

BY WHAT SHALL WE MEASURE?

A little tree, short, but self-satisfied,
Glanced toward the ground, then tossed its head, and cried,
"Behold, how tall I am, how far the earth!"
And boasting thus, it swayed in scornful mirth.

The tallest pine tree in the forest raised
Its head toward heaven, and sighed the while it gazed;
"Alas, how small I am, and the great skies how far,
What years of space 'twixt me and yonder star."

Our height depends on what we measure by—
If up from earth or downward from the sky.[21]

TREES ARE SPECIAL FRIENDS

What is *your* tree? A pine with slim, long, tapering stem and dark needle-clusters borne on horizontally stretching limbs? An old oak with sturdy trunk, and a spreading crown built with a framework of branches and twigs—knotted, gnarled, criss-crossing and upward-curving? An elm tree, tall and graceful and spraying out, fountainlike? Or some other quite different tree? . . .

Thoreau sensed the special and consistent character of the forms of trees of different species. He has pointed out that in some species the branches start low on the trunk; in some they are far above the ground; in some they grow with fairly even or proportioned spacing along nearly the whole length of a tapering, mid-rib trunk-stem; in some they make endlessly the letter *Y*, from lower trunk to topmost twig. He saw that the branches of certain trees are nearly horizontal; in some they droop; in others they tend to spring upward. On his walks he drew in his notebooks, without trained skill, simple, true little sketches of familiar tree-types to illustrate these differences. . . . Japanese art with its traditional simplicity has reduced tree-forms to a few essential strokes which the Japanese painter or draughtsman must accept as his rule. . . .

Tree form pervades nature. We find it not only in all plant life but also in the systems of arteries and veins in animals, in antlers, in corals; we find it in crystal formations and in river systems. Tree-form outlines are used by science commonly in making graphic representations of the evolution and classification of the plants and animals of the world. The term "family tree" is familiar to everyone. . . .

Walt Whitman said: "Why are there trees I never walk under, but large and melodious thoughts descend upon me?" And elsewhere . . . "How the trees rise and stand up—with strong trunks—with branches and leaves! (Surely there is something more in each of the trees—some living Soul.)" From Thoreau, poet-naturalist-philosopher, we have: "The pines impress me as human. . . . Nothing in this world stands up more free from blame than a pine tree." . . .

Whether with the poets, artists, and philosophers we feel a tree, or with the scientists gain some idea of the structure and work of a tree, the resultant for us in either case is, perhaps, a sense of wonder and reverence that such a thing can be. Trees have been called nature's utmost success in the development of a plant. They have sturdiness and long life; they embody an amazing range of diversified forms and textures in their many parts; they have transcendent and changing beauty; they afford limitless uses to mankind; they have manufacturing and evaporation systems which are marvels to the engineer, as well as to the botanist.[22]

TO THE WAYFARER

Ye who pass by and would raise your hand against me,
Hearken ere you harm me!
I am the heat of your hearth on the cold winter nights,
The friendly shade screening you from the summer sun.
My fruits are refreshing drafts,

Quenching your thirst as you journey on.
I am the beam that holds your house,
The board of your table,
The bed on which you lie,
And the timber that builds your boat.
I am the handle of your hoe,
The door of your homestead.
I am the wood of your cradle,
And the shell of your coffin.
I am the bread of kindness, and the flower of beauty.
Ye who pass by, listen to my prayer: harm me not.[23]

THE STRENGTH OF THE TREE

The tree is tremendously alive.

How implacable it stands. How marvelous is its growth. How deep the great roots burrow into the soil, there carefully to select the elements which shall nourish it and bring the whole tree to a splendid assertion of life. The great tree draws strength from the Lord God, from his rich soil and clear air and warm sunlight. In quiet and serene wisdom it grows strong by taking from God the nourishment which he has provided.

The psalmist found the tree to be a parable of the possibilities of human life (Psalm 1). Meditate upon these thoughts: Do not I need to live quietly and serenely like the tree . . . to put my hands into the good earth . . . to look up at the clear sky . . . to live by the law of God and to meditate upon it day and night? . . . Then may I achieve the natural strength and beauty and usefulness of the tree. Meditate upon those experiences which give you strength and beauty, and those experiences which sap your vital energy. . . .

Now pray . . . finishing your prayer in these words:

Almighty God, in whom I live and move and have my being, grant me the wisdom to depend more fully upon thee. Prompt me to put forth my hands to take the nourishment which thou hast provided for my welfare. Help me carefully to select, among all the varied experiences which are open to me, only those that are in harmony with thy will. Help me to become as certain in this wisdom as the tree. So shall I grow and prosper like the tree as I rest my life upon thy never-failing strength. Amen.[24]

WHEN THE STARS COME OUT

The most important thing about the stars to most of us who know very little about them is their beauty. But there is more to the stars than beauty. There is great mystery that has made men of every age study the stars for their secrets; there is order that affects the life of each of us; there are some of the most interesting stories in the world illustrated with pictures drawn by the stars. In ancient times the stars were worshipped as gods. . . . Men known as astrologers spent their lives in trying to learn the secrets of the stars. They believed they could foretell events by the movements of the heavenly bodies. . . .

The sky was the first clock for mankind. As the earth moved—though early peoples did not know the earth moved—the face of the sky would change. Different groups of stars would appear at certain times, and thus time and seasons were recognized.

The moon affected the tides of the great waters of the world and the stars pointed out directions. The Egyptians laid out their famous pyramids and began the science of surveying by their knowledge of the North Star and its relationship to other stars.

As the magic-study called astrology gave way to the science-study called astronomy, new things were learned about the stars.

Men learned that every shining star they saw in the heavens was a sun, most of them bigger than our own.

They found out that the stars are so far away that they could not be measured in miles, as we measure things on the earth. So they had to invent a new unit of distance, the "light" year. . . .

But if you would like to hear some of the distances in miles, try to imagine these:

The sun is ninety-three million miles away—and you remember that the diameter of the earth itself is less than eight thousand miles. But the sun is a moving star; the next nearest star is twenty thousand times as far away from the sun as the earth is.

Neptune, one of the planets in our solar system, is almost three thousand million miles from the sun. . . .

Suppose the sun were the size of a two-foot globe. If it were, the earth would be the size of a green pea, and the planet Mars would be the size of a pin head. But little Mercury would be no bigger than a mustard seed. . . .

The stars have been shining down on the earth for thousands or millions of years. . . . Nations rise and fall, floods and wars come and go, but those stars keep shining down.

Do you see how small it makes us seem? . . .

What if there were no law of gravity? We should be thrown off in a second, and go tumbling through space.

What if two of the planets should crash? Have you ever thought how wonderful it is that, as much as they spin around through space at such high rates of speed, they always keep their own course, even though we can't see anything that keeps them there? . . .

Can you imagine anything planned by man working out so marvelously?

And we begin to wonder what it's all about, and whether perhaps all our talk of a God who is concerned with each one of us is really true, or whether it's just a sign of egotism. . . . Maybe we're no more important to God than some little insect is to us.

But then we remember something we had forgotten.

Our bodies are small, and our lives on earth are short, but we have been given souls and minds that make us ask such questions. Man's spirit is kin to God and is greater than anything in the universe. . . .

And as we think over the question of how God could be concerned with such tiny pinpoints as ourselves, the idea turns to this: God, who created this mighty universe, and who guides it with forces which we not only cannot see but cannot even understand, created man. He created man with a longing for God, with a desire to learn the secrets of the universe, with a soul which has made us insist from the beginning of the world that man cannot completely die. . . .

And then we see another power in ourselves that is left out in the laws of the physical universe. We can decide for ourselves what we shall do. The great truths about us point to what will happen if we do a certain thing, but unlike the stars which move in fixed orbits, we set our own paths. . . .

Man is insignificant but mighty, and the stars which shine down on us may make us realize what a small part each of us is in the universe, but they also show us the might and power of a God who has created us with understanding and a desire for communion with him.[25]

EVENING STAR

Evening star up yonder,
  Teach me like you to wander
Willing and obediently
  The path that God ordained for me!
Evening star up yonder!

Teach me, gentle flowers,
  To wait for springtime showers.
In this winter world to grow,
  Green and strong beneath the snow,
Teach me, gentle flowers.

Mighty ocean, teach me,
  To do the task that needs me,
And reflect as days depart,
  Heaven's peace within my heart,
Mighty ocean, teach me.

Shady lanes, refreshing,
  Teach me to be a blessing,
To some weary soul each day,
  Friends or foes who pass my way,
Shady lanes, refreshing.

Evening sun, descending,
  Teach me, when life is ending,
Night shall pass, and I like you,
  Shall rise again, where life is new,
Teach me, sun descending.[26]

MICHAEL PUPIN'S HEAVENLY LANGUAGE

Fifty years ago, instructed by David's psalms, I found in the light of the stars a heavenly language which proclaims the glory of God, but I did not know how that language reached me, and I hoped that some day I might find out. That hope was in my soul when I landed at Castle Garden. Today science tells me that the stars themselves bring it to me. Each burning star is a focus of energy, of life-giving activity, which it pours out lavishly into every direction of the energy-hungry space; it pours out the life of its own heart, in order to beget new life. Oh, what a beautiful vista that opens to our imagination, and what new beauties are disclosed by science in the meaning of the words in Genesis: "He breathed into his nostrils the breath of life, and man became a living soul." The light of the stars is a part of the life-giving breath of God. I never look now upon the starlight vault of heaven without feeling this divine breath and its quickening action upon my soul.[27]

A GARDEN PSALM

My garden brings me near to Thee, O God, Creator of all things.

Only God can make a tree.
Only God can make a dewdrop.

When I see dewdrops touched by rays of rising sun sparkling like jewels hanging pendent on grass blades or graceful shrubs, or tracing spider webs with iridescent beauty;
When I ponder upon the miracle of tiny seeds planted and nourished by earth and rain and sun and air, growing day by day, then making a mist of color at which I may gaze in wonder and delight, I know this is Thy handiwork, O God.

Thou hast made the birds for the trees and trees for the birds: boughs for them to perch upon to sing songs so thrilling as almost to burst the feathered throats.

Thou hast made a carpet of grass to lie spread out in luxuriant softness and refreshing green.
By my labor I help to produce fruit of vine and bush and tree, which nourishes the body and brings satisfaction to the soul.[28]

WHEN WE HAVE "SEEING EYES"

Our little verse, "All things bright and beautiful . . ." ends with the line, "Our Father made them all." As we have heard of and seen these beautiful creations, our minds have been turned toward the Maker of them. Somehow, to really see these things is to behold the beauty of the Lord, for the closer we come to knowing and appreciating the wonders of God's world, the more we know of him. We start down a path of discovery of flowers or trees or creatures, and find ourselves on a path to God. "A thing of beauty is a joy forever," the poet sings. It is a joy forever for it is a constant reminder of the Father, of his love and care for us and for all his creations. And so "seeing eyes" will lead us into seeing God the Father, whom we may glorify and enjoy forever.[29]

OVERTONES

Over the ground is a mat of green,
Over the green the dew;
Over the dew are the arching trees;
Over the trees the blue.
Dotting the blue are the scudding clouds;
Over the clouds the sun;
Over the sun is the love of God,
Brooding us every one.[30]

GROWING LIFE ABOUT US ALL THE TIME

. . . Because they have wondered about the growth taking place within the seed, the leaf bud which will appear near the scar the old leaf left, the winged loveliness which will burst forth from the dull-looking cocoon, the scattered atoms which will find their way to the arrangement we call a crystal, or the formless invisible vapor which under exact conditions will become a globule of dew, children will listen responsively to Whitman's lines where he says:

> The universe is duly in order, everything is in
>   its place,
> What has arrived is in its place, and what waits
>   is in its place.[31]

THE PASSING OF DAY

Day has such a lovely way of going;
The moon and stars wait quietly, and then
They steal across the silent sky. The glen
Is calm—does it have a way of knowing,
Of feeling, that He above is sowing
On the earth seeds that govern fearing men?

Off in the lonely shadows pipes a wren,
Joyous song that sets the heart a-glowing.
Such sounds and sights of wonder stir the heart;
Often I search my mind for just one word
To help describe these wonders of God's art.

The trees a vigil through the night will keep;
The stir of leaves may now and then be heard
But once again, the world is lost in sleep.[32]

PRAISE GOD FOR SOIL

Psalms 24:1a

Look down at your feet. What do you see there—grass, or vines, dead leaves? But underneath, what then—the soil, the good earth. For when our Bible refers to the earth sometimes it means the world and all that is in it, but often it means the soil. And that is right, for without soil, there could be no world, no earth.

If you can, reach down and get a handful of earth and hold it in your hand. It is not really dirty, although it is often called dirt, for it is moist, it is cool, and within it is life for man and plants and the animals of the world. It is holy earth.

Genesis 1:1

God created the earth, so that the roots of plants might grow down into it. Because of this earth the roots are able to hold upright the plants themselves, a stalk of wheat, or a great Sequoia tree. Through it the roots take in moisture and minerals to help the plants manufacture food for themselves, for animals, and for man. Surely this earth, then, is holy.

And the earth which you as a camper in Georgia pick up is different from the earth which the camper in Tennessee, or Texas, or Oregon, may pick up. It may be a different color; it probably grows different crops; but without it none of you could exist. Praise God for the holy earth!

What makes a topsoil rich, able to produce food for man and beast? It is the humus which is made up of the decayed plants and animals which have died. So continues the cycle of the holy earth. It feeds and nurtures plants and animals, who, when they are no longer alive again, go back to enrich the earth.

How long did it take God to make the precious topsoil? Men who have studied the subject say that it took five hundred years to make an inch of it. Thus, if there are only six inches of topsoil the Creator worked three thousand years to make it. And the rich eighteen inches of some parts of Iowa took God nine thousand years to make.

Just as you have held in the soil in your hands, so man holds all the soil of the earth in his hands. That is the way God planned it. God meant that man should till the soil and produce food for himself and for others, for that is the way God made the world. But do you think he meant that man should till it carelessly, exposing it to the wind and the rain, so that it washes downhill and makes silt in the streams, even filling up with silt the reservoirs which man himself has made? Man working with God can hold in place the rich topsoil and make it richer. Man working against God can make barren hillsides and silted streams.

Take up again your handful of earth and think carefully about it. . . .[33]

THE ELEVENTH COMMMANDMENT

Thou shalt inherit the holy earth as a faithful steward, conserving its resources and productivity from generation to generation. Thou shalt safeguard thy fields from soil erosion, thy living waters from drying up, thy forests from desolation, and protect thy hills from overgrazing by thy herds, that thy descendants may have abundance forever. If any shall fail in this stewardship of the land thy fruitful fields shall become sterile stony ground and wasting gullies, and thy descendants shall decrease and live in poverty or perish from off the face of the earth.[34]

10

God's One-World Family and Our Part in Building Brotherhood

THE DAY BEGINS

In the sweet solitude of early morning hours
When first the sun with earth the day's communion takes,
Breathes a still voice that asks in accents pleading,
"This day of yours—what of it will you make?"

Then from the heart a cry
"Oh God, what shall I do
To keep thee close beside
And to thy will be true?"

An answer echoing comes
"Thyself thou must forget—
Be mine. Remember when thou
Diest I shall be living yet.
I am the law of Love,
The magic key of life,
Lying at your side.
Be strong, forget yourself

To live and love and build
God knows the time for all.
Then feel not blind
If within your heart you trim
The Inner Light. Then forward step
Glad, free, and unafraid." [1]

MY BODY IS HOLY

My body is the temple of my soul. Therefore;
I will keep my body clean within and without.
I will breathe pure air and I will live in the sunlight.
I will do no act that might endanger the health of others.
I will try to learn and practice the rules of healthful living.
I will work and rest and play at the right times and in the right way, so that my mind may be strong and my body healthy, and so that I may lead a useful life and be an honor to my parents, to my friends, and to my country.[2]

MY HAND

This hand of mine is a wonderful piece of machinery—a queer looking thing, when you examine it closely—just a flat object with extensions, octopus fashion, radiating from it. Soft to touch, yet underneath a bony structure. There is blood, a deep red, healing fluid, flowing to the very tips of these fingers and back again.

This hand of mine can move without any outside force. I say "close up" and the fingers curl into a fist. I say "open" and they stretch taut—nor do I have to say this aloud. One finger, two fingers, three fingers, can obey my thinking. That chair cannot move. I can scream and yell, yet each leg and arm and the back remain motionless. It hasn't in it those intricate muscles and nerve fibers bound together in a way that makes it a machine all by itself.

The Inventor of this machine has a mind far beyond mine—for, though the machine belongs to me, I do not understand it—nor, given complete control of it, would I know how to keep its parts in running order. So I must rely constantly on that Inventor to keep the blood coursing, the skin growing, the nerves feeling. I wonder why he made that hand! And why he put that hand on me? Who am I that I should have custody of such a wonderful machine? It can do things—hold a clod of earth and touch the sky. It can make things—which fly through the air, to destroy or bring together. It can push a person—or lift. It can twist and destroy—or it can heal. It can get or give. I wonder why the Inventor made that hand! If I could discover that, and he and I could work together, there is no end to what that hand could do.[3]

NOTHING LESS THAN PERFECT

Here is a fragment of an old play about a master workman who did even the smallest things well:

THE DUKE (*To man at work in the Palazzo Vecchio*): How come you here?

THE MAN: I await my companions, sire.

THE DUKE: Ah, the frescoes; yes. And the box you are making for pastime, how will it be used?

THE MAN: Flowers will be planted in it, sire.

THE DUKE: It will be filled with dirt. Why take such pains with it, to make each joint and surface perfect?

THE MAN: I love perfect things.

THE DUKE: Eh? It is wasted effort. No one will observe its perfection. Its usage does not require such perfection.

THE MAN: But my spirit does.
THE DUKE (*Scowling*): Sirrah, what?
THE MAN: Do you suppose that the Carpenter of Nazareth ever made anything less well than He could? That He was ever satisfied with anything less perfect than it could be made?
THE DUKE (*Angrily*): Sacrilege! Fellow, you shall be flogged. What is your name?
THE MAN: Michelangelo, sire.[4]

BEATITUDES FOR CAMPERS

Happy are they that have deep insight:
They shall rejoice in undiscovered ways of God.

Happy are they who sing soulful songs:
They carry light and joy to shadowed lives.
Happy are they who know the power of love:
They live in his spirit, for God is love.

Happy are they that live for truth:
They find a way to relieve the hearts of men.
Happy are the souls fully given to thee:
They shall be filled with peace and perfect love.[5]

CHINESE FOLK SAYING

When the sun rises, I go to work;
When the sun goes down, I take my rest;
I dig the well from which I drink;
I farm the soil that yields my food.
I share creation; kings do no more.[6]

INDIAN FOLK SAYING

In beauty I walk,
With beauty before me I walk,

With beauty behind me I walk,
With beauty above me I walk.[7]

TEN COMMANDMENTS OF SPORTSMANSHIP

Thou shalt finish the game thou beginnest.
Thou shalt take losses without excuses.
Thou shalt be humble in victory.
Thou shalt honor the referee or umpire.
Thou shalt share the glory of winning with thy teammates.
Thou shalt be willing to give thine opponent every advantage thou askest.
Thou shalt play for the sake of the game and the joy of playing.
Thou shalt do team work unselfishly.
Thou shalt honor the game.[8]

BEING CLEAN

Be clean. As a habit of life this will pay dividends in personal satisfaction. He who thinks he can be crooked and "get away with it" has yet much to learn of comparative value. Here, however, keeping clean is presented rather as a practical business asset whose value is being insisted upon with a daily increasing sharpness.

Clean is an adjective of vast import. It attaches no less to the mind which prompts than to the body which performs. "A Good Clean Man" is often the endorsement on which he wins out. Standards in all lives are steadily advancing and each advance makes the "going" just so much the harder for those who fail to meet them.

In maintaining a social balance, a person must consider what particular personal qualities are looked upon with favor by the public. Society looks for evidence of good taste partly through appearance, cleanliness, neatness, and use of good language. Society also values dependability, loyalty, honesty, and truthfulness. Honesty in a person means that he can be trusted, that he does not resort to crookedness in achieving his goals. When a person has a clean mind he is usually truthful and honest in what he says. He is usually spoken of as a clean-living person of high ideals.[9]

ON WATCH FOR LITTLE THINGS

A ship was once wrecked on the Irish coast. The captain was a careful one. Nor had the weather been of so severe a kind as to explain the wide distance to which the vessel had swerved from her proper course. The ship went down. Among other portions of the vessel that were examined was the compass that was swung on deck, and inside the compass-box was detected a bit of steel, which appeared to be the small point of a pocket-knife blade. It appeared that the day before the wreck a sailor had been sent to clean the compass, had used his pocket-knife in the process, and had unconsciously broken off the point and left it remaining in the box. That bit of knife-blade exerted its influence on the compass, and to a degree that deflected the needle from its proper bent. That piece of knife wrecked the ship.

For want of a nail, a shoe was lost.
For want of a shoe, a horse was lost.
For want of a horse, a message was lost.
For want of a message, a battle was lost.
For want of a battle, a Kingdom was lost.

Little meannesses, little faults, little lies, little bad habits, little slips, little sins: all can turn our lives aside. We ought to be on the alert for them all the time.

But it is also true that little things of the right sort can make our lives much better. Little words of encouragement, little acts of kindness and thoughtfulness, little resolutions for truth and courage, little prayers said with honesty: all these can build a good life.

After this, when you say, "Aw, that's nuthin'," be careful what you are saying it about.[10]

TEMPER

Read Ephesians 4:25-32. Think of the word "Temper"—

This word is badly used among us. We usually make it mean that flaring-up of emotion when we lost control of ourselves. Most of the time "Temper" means something we are sorry for after we let go.

But that is not the real meaning at all. Temper is a quality of fine steel. Did you ever hear of the famous Damascus swords of ancient times, or the almost equally famous Toledo blades of the Middle Ages? The masters of the art of tempering steel made them, and they were eagerly sought after all over the world. By a secret process of using heat they were able to produce swords strong enough to put through steel and sharp enough to cut silk floating in the air. The whole trick was the use of heat at the right time and in the right way.

Now we all know what it is to "burn up." We wouldn't be worth much if we didn't. But what does it do to us? How do we handle it? Does almost anything set us off? Do we let ourselves be "touchy," so that everyone else has to walk cautiously to avoid our wrath?

Here's a tip on the use of all that heat. The secret, as with the fine swords, is to use the heat at the right time and place. If you will learn to "burn up" only about things that do a wrong to other people, you will have a temper worth having. Don't waste any of it on yourself. Notice the fact that Jesus was too big for any kind of resentment toward anything mean people might do to him. He was too big to be bothered by it. But when he saw someone strong oppressing someone weaker, he "burned up." . . . But it was always controlled, and he was always master of himself.

Prayer: Father, temper our spirits. Teach us to save our fire for thy service and not for our own. Amen.[11]

THE SELF I MIGHT BECOME

An artist, seeking a quiet place to rest, came to a little village nestled high among the mountains. There he stayed with the humble, friendly people. After a while, he ventured out to a level ledge overlooking the hills. Quietly he painted. Occasionally one of the village boys and girls or older people would serve as models. He was not a talkative fellow; and the understanding villagers did not pry into his affairs with questions.

Then another stranger came to the village. The artist could tell that he looked sad, almost despairing. His shoulders drooped, and in his face there was no look of hope. Soon rumors went about that this stranger had once been very successful and popular.

The artist began working quickly with his paints and canvas; he was painting the man without his knowing it. This was to be his masterpiece.

Finally, the painting was finished and veiled. The artist, almost with breathless eagerness, invited the man to come with him to see a painting. The man wondered why he should have been the one invited, but having nothing better to do, he went. He seemed pathetically grateful that someone had noticed him and offered a friendly gesture. Together, then, they went to the studio. The artist with one quick gesture unveiled the painting.

The stranger stood aghast. Could it be? No! It couldn't be—but it was!—himself there! That man in the picture, however, was standing erect, unafraid, a light of high purpose in his eyes. The stranger looked again. He squared his shoulders. His face began to light up, for new hope had come into his heart. He went out a new man. Despite the difficulties he had known, he was going to try again.

Prayer: O Father God, when we miss Your plan and fail, help us to see ourselves as You see us; may we try again a new best.[12]

11

Our Lives in God's Plan and Our Call to Live at Our Best

PRAYER OF BOY WHO DID NOT KNOW HOW TO BE A PART OF A GROUP

Dear Lord:

Many times when I could have helped someone else I was doing things for my own enjoyment. Many times when I could have given a helping hand to someone in need, I did not. I was afraid of being scoffed at. Many times when I should have shared things with others I did not because I was too selfish. Many times I have made fun of people for things they could not help, because I am "smart." Many times I have not admitted my mistakes because I was too proud. Many times I have sulked when I was corrected because I think I "know it all." Many times I have snubbed people because I thought I was too good for them.

Please forgive me of these and many other sins I have committed. Amen.[1]

THE GIFT OF FRIENDSHIP

I think that God will never send
A gift so precious as a friend—
A friend who always understands
And fills each need as it demands;
Whose loyalty will stand the test,
When skies are bright or overcast,
Who sees the faults that merit blame
But keeps on loving just the same;
Who does far more than creeds could do
To make us good, to make us true.[2]

CAMPERS TELL THE GOOD SAMARITAN STORY

A certain boy went down from Detroit to Camp Ohiyesa and fell among selfish, unfriendly boys, who robbed him of his good times, made fun of his handicaps, tormented him, and departed, leaving him miserable and half sick with loneliness. And by chance there came down a certain counselor that way, and when he saw him he passed by on the other side. And likewise a cabinet member, when he was at the place, came and looked on him, but being concerned for his own work and comfort, passed by on the other side. But a certain Polish boy, little known in camp and a stranger to the unhappy lad, as he played, came where he was; and when he saw him, he had compassion on him, and went to him, and bound up the wounds of loneliness, pouring in sympathy and friendliness, and set him in his own boat, and took him out rowing, and cheered him. And at the end of the ride when he departed, he took out half a candy bar, and gave it to him, and said unto him, "Take this: and if you want me for a friend, tomorrow when I come again, I will play with you."

Which one of these three, thinkest thou, was neighbour unto him that fell among the selfish boys?[3]

MAKING MY CAMP A "COMMUNITY"

A community is a group of people who seek the welfare of all its members. A Christian community is a group of people who love God and each other in such a way that they seek the spirit of Jesus in their day-to-day living with each other.

Here are some of the ways in which you may help to make this camp a Christian community. Read all of them slowly. Then check with your pencil two you will try especially to do during this camping season.

1. I will seek each day to talk with God.
2. I will help clean up camp so that the camp will be a happier place for all of us.
3. I will try to look on every camper as an important person who has something to give the camp which I may not have.
4. I will share my ideas and thoughts with my group. I may think of something no one else thinks of.
5. I will learn to work with others for the good of all.
6. I will learn to listen and to look for things which the out-of-doors may say to me about God.
7. I will help finish the things we begin.

Now you cannot do these things by yourself. God wants to help you do them. Other campers and counselors can help also.

Read Acts 1:8.

Think with God about these ideas.[4]

GOD'S ONE-WORLD FAMILY

In the Hebrew hymnbook there is a song of the nations. Turn in your Bible to Psalm 117 and read it. What does praise mean? Read it again, and substitute "families" for "peoples." Is the meaning different now? How does God show His loving-kindness to all the peoples who live on the earth, and not only to America?

In order to bring happiness to all people, the families of the earth must learn to have fellowship with one another.

Now the United Nations is one effort to bring the families of the world into one big family. The times it has failed are times when nations acted selfishly instead of for the good of all.

The World Council of Churches is another effort. But the World Council says that it does not know what unselfishness is until it measures its own selfishness by God's selflessness. We can act in a brotherly way only when our loyalty becomes to One higher than a nation, or family, or race.

To the meetings of the World Council go church people from the nations of the world. . . . Your junior high camp is a part of the world-wide church. . . . To it came boys and girls from many families and many churches. The shelter families tried to learn to live happily with other shelter families until the camp became one big family.

Would you like to think with God, now that you are going home, of all the boys and girls you met at camp? (*Pause; prayer.*)

Would you like to pray that your own church may be a better member of the world church family? (*Pause; prayer.*)

Would you like to pray that you may live as a member of the world Christian community? (*Pause; prayer.*)[5]

I BELIEVE IN MY FAR-AWAY FRIEND

I believe in my far-away friend.
He is the boy I have not yet come to know well.
Perhaps he is a boy I have never learned to know at all.
He may be on the other side of the world, or in a skin of a different color than mine. He may come from a wealthier family than mine, or poorer.
Just what sort of a boy he is, in every way, I cannot say.
Yet I believe in him.
Somehow I can see that he is much the same boy that I am, even though he seems to be different.
He plays and works, worries and rests, dreams of the future, and gets restless at the present, just as I do,
He and I may never actually meet—yet we will touch each other in many ways.
The clothes one of us wears, or the corn he raises, or the coffee he grows, or the spices he carries to market, or the cotton he gathers, will go across many miles to supply the needs of the other.[6]

OUR WORLD

For this world of Thine so big and wide
Yet all athrob with beauty
For the perfect form of every flower,
The golden hush of the sunset hour
For Thy changeless order ever new
With one great purpose all shot through,
We thank Thee, God, for a world so big!

For this world of ours so cramped and cruel
And split with war and strife;

For starving children, breaking hearts,
That mass who move by jerks and starts;
For growing hate, distorted truth,
That broken dream of eager youth—
Forgive us, Lord, for a world so small!

For a world as big as Thy dreams, O God,
We deeply, truly pray;
For a world where races are but one
And love reaches out as the rays of the sun,
Where everyone has a chance to grow,
And earth shall feel Thy Spirit's flow,
We pray Thee, God, enlarge our world! [7]

THE OCEAN JOINS FRIENDS

The water creeps toward us
Now quietly and gently,
Now suddenly and loud.
What sound is it we hear
From the home of the sea animals?

We move away;
It comes again
Lashing our feet
Then running back between the sand.

I think it is God speaking
To say an African boy
Out there has his feet in the sand
Facing this way.

A thousand miles away he is.
Then I dive into the water to meet the waves
And he comes as near to me as I think.[8]

THINGS SO BEAUTIFUL AND LOVING

The woods were so big
The green leaves
And the little flowers.
I wondered how God could even think of things
So beautiful
And loving.[9]

AMERICA

God built Him a continent of glory and filled it with treasures untold;
He carpeted it with soft-rolling prairies and columned it with thundering mountains;
He studded it with sweet-flowing fountains and traced it with long-winding streams;
He planted it with deep-shadowed forests, and filled them with song.

Then He called unto a thousand peoples and summoned the bravest among them.
They came from the ends of the earth, each bearing a gift and a hope.
The glow of adventure was in their eyes, and in their hearts the glory of hope.

And out of the bounty of earth and the labor of men,
Out of the longing of hearts and the prayer of souls,
Out of the memory of ages and the hopes of the world,
God fashioned a nation in love, blessed it with a purpose sublime—
And called it AMERICA! [10]

PARENTS ARE FRIENDS

Read Exodus 20:12; Proverbs 10:1

Sometimes we have to be without things to appreciate them. We take too easily for granted those who are around us every day. How much we need to learn about our fathers and mothers, and the others in our families! They have always been there, and we haven't thought very much about how much we owe them. In the helplessness of our infancy, they cared for us. As we have grown up they have protected us from the things that would harm us, but gradually let us have more and more freedom.

And the joys of brothers and sisters. That may make us smile for a moment when we remember the grand and glorious scraps we have with them. But life without them would be awfully lonely.

We are old enough now to ask ourselves whether we are doing our part. Is life at home going to be easier for everyone when we get back from camp? Are we going to show our parents that we appreciate their love and sacrifice, by doing better in school, by obeying more cheerfully, by putting something into the whole life of the home? And while we are here are we acting so that others will say, "That boy must come from a fine home"?

When John G. Paton, who afterwards became a great missionary, was leaving home, his father walked with him for several miles, and when they had to part, the father said, "God bless you, son! Your father's God prosper you and keep you from all evil." When some distance was between them John looked back, and saw his father still watching him. Afterwards he said, "Hastening on my way, I vowed deeply and oft, by the help of God, to live and to act so as never to grieve or dishonor such a father and mother as He had given me." [11]

THE INVINCIBLE LEADER

"Tell me a story about when you were a great soldier. Tell me about one of the battles you won," said a little boy to his grandfather.

The old man had been a colonel in the Austrian army for many years and could recount fierce tales of conquest by his troops. But today he shook his head as he took the boy upon his knee.

"I will tell you, instead," he said, "of the greatest battle I ever lost, which was won by braver men than mine."

The little boy was astonished, for he thought that his grandfather's soldiers were the bravest in the world. So he listened eagerly.

"I was commanded," the old colonel began, "to march against a little town in the Tyrol and lay siege to it. We had been meeting stubborn resistance in that part of the country, but we felt that we should win because all of the advantages were on our side. My confidence, however, was arrested by a remark from a prisoner we had taken. 'You will never take that town,' he said, 'for they have an Invincible Leader.'

" 'What does the fellow mean?' I inquired of one of my staff. 'And who is this leader of whom he speaks?'

"Nobody seemed able to answer my question, and so in case there should be some truth in the report, I doubled preparations.

"As we descended through the pass in the Alps, I saw with surprise that the cattle were still grazing in the valley and that women and children—yes, and even men—were working in the fields.

" 'Either they were not expecting us, or this is a trap to catch us,' I thought to myself. As we drew nearer the town we passed people on the road. They smiled and greeted us with a friendly word, and then went on their way. So friendly was their attitude toward us, and so different from the usual reception given us, that my soldiers forgot they were under discipline and returned the greeting.

"Finally we reached the town and clattered up the cobble-paved streets—colors flying, horns sounding a challenge, arms in readiness. The forge of the blacksmith shop was glowing, and the smith left it to stand in the door with a number of others to watch us pass. Suddenly he waved to one of my soldiers and I heard him exclaim, 'I knew that fellow when we were boys together at Innsbruck!'

"Women came to the windows or doorways with little babies in their arms. Some of them looked startled and held the babies closer, then went quickly on with their household tasks without panic or confusion. As for the boys—little fellows like you, my son," the old man cuddled the boy in his arms; "they made us feel as though we were taking part in a glorious parade for their special amusement. They swarmed after us, whooping with delight and asking innumerable questions about the weapons we carried. Apparently they had never seen guns and swords before.

"It was impossible to keep strict discipline, and I began to feel rather foolish. My soldiers answered the questions of the children, and I saw the old warrior throw a kiss to a little golden-haired tot on a doorstep. 'Just the size of my Lisa,' he muttered.

"Still no sign of an ambush. We rode straight to the open square on which faced the town hall. Here, if anywhere, resistance was to be expected. This is what we found. The door of the beautiful old building was wide open. Pigeons flew up from the grass around the fountain as we approached. No cannon or barricade was in sight, and my regiment, as it poured into the square, looked out of place.

"Just as I had reached the hall and my guard was drawn up at attention, an old white-haired man, who by his insignia I surmised to be the mayor, stepped forth, followed by ten men in simple peasants' costume. They were all dignified and unabashed by the armed force before them—the most terrible soldiers of the great army of Austria."

"And what did this old man say, in the face of your guns and your cannon?" asked the little boy breathlessly.

"He walked down the steps, straight to my horse's side, and with hand extended, cried, 'Welcome, brother!' One of my aides made a gesture as if to strike him down with his sword, but I saw by the face of the old mayor that this was no trick on his part.

" 'Where are your soldiers?' I demanded.

" 'Soldiers? Why, don't you know we have none?' he replied in wonderment, as though I had said, 'Where are your giants?' or 'Where are your dwarfs?'

" 'But we have come to take the town.'

" 'Well, no one will stop you.'

" 'Are there none here to fight?'

"At this question, the old man's face lit up with a rare smile that I will always remember. Often afterwards, when engaged in bloody warfare, I would suddenly see that man's smile—and somehow, I came to hate my business. His words were simple: 'No, there is no one here to fight. We have chosen Christ for our Leader, and he taught men another way.' "

"What did you do then, grandfather?" asked the little boy eagerly.

"Do you know, son," the old soldier answered, "there seemed nothing left for us to do but to ride away, leaving the town unmolested. It was impossible to take it. If I had ordered my soldiers to fire on those smiling men, women, and children, I know they would not have obeyed me. Even military discipline has its limits. Could I command the grisly soldier to shoot down the child who reminded him of his Lisa? I reported to headquarters that the town had offered unassailable resistance, although this admission injured my military reputation. But I was right. We had literally been conquered by these simple folk, who followed implicitly the leadership of Jesus Christ." [12]

SPEAKING FOR THE UNITED NATIONS

JACK (*fervently*): It means everything to me [this chance to talk to representatives of all the great religions of the world meeting with a common purpose]. And it should mean that much to you . . . to everybody. And that's what I'm going to tell them. Thanks to your visit, I have something definite to say now. I'm no great philosopher or poet—they certainly deserve a grander voice than mine, but I'm going to let them know that young people believe in the dignity and goodness of man and the word of God. I'm going to speak for—for the ordinary man who never gets a chance to speak for himself to people like these. I'm going to stand up there for people everywhere who pray and hope for the United

Nations and its triumph. They'll hear me and they'll know that common people the world over encourage, support, and bless them in their fine work.

NARRATOR (*slowly building*): The spotlight may be on me—

But you are being watched.
The martyrs and the saints,
Men of God everywhere,
Men living, men long gone—
They are watching.
Prophets and poets—
Simple and faithful men,
Great spirits of humanity,
All their eyes are on you . . .
All their hearts are with you.
Confucius . . .
Buddha Gautama . . .
Lao Tse and Moses . . .
Mohammed . . .
Jesus—
They are watching, they are praying for you,
And you must do what is in your hearts.
[*Pause*]
Make history in this hall.
Make history that will brighten the world with hope
With love and peace.
Make it for the wretched millions who are despairing in these dark, bitter days.
Make history.
Make history bend skywards, skywards to God.
Change the course we're on now.
The world deserves a chance to survive.
And you, men of God from everywhere,

You are fortunate, you are privileged to lead the rest of the world to universal love and peace.
[*Pause*]
It is no easy mission.
Your enemies are powerful. The Godless in this world
Are confident that you shall fail, that the United Nations shall fail. The same brute who tramples on human rights wants the light of God's truth to dim and dim and die out.
So many don't even dare to hope for peace in these dark times.
Your task is to provide the basis for that hope to grow again.
Human brotherhood in full size
Will be an impenetrable mountain of truth.
You can make history bend upwards to God
And God is watching you, I know.

This play should end with a prayer—
But it would be repetitious, you see.
For in its crude way this whole presentation
Has been a prayer. The whole cause of the United Nations is a prayer uttered by a planet groping for the peace that must surely come.
The United Nations is a prayer uttered by a street-urchin standing in a doorway in Naples . . .
by a farmer on the western plains of Canada . . .
by a soldier in the Palestine hills . . .
by a baker in Capetown . . .
by a steel-worker in Pittsburgh . . .
by a fisherman on the upper Yangtze . . .
by a young mother in Bombay . . .
by all of us in this hall.[13]

GOODNIGHT!

Come all—Sing goodnight,
While the shadows creep into evening light.
In each living, glowing ember
There are friendships to remember.
So we'll sing one last goodnight!
Goodnight! Goodnight! [14]

12

Prayers

SAVE ME FROM HATING PEOPLE

Lord of all love, let there march before my eyes now the people whom I find it so easy to hate.

The men and women of the countries with which my nation has been at war,—show me them, my Lord.

Those whom I distrust in the nations that have fought beside my own,—let me see these, O God.

My neighbors whose ideas I do not like,—dare I overlook these, thou Father of my spirit?

Grant thou unto me, Lord of all love, a warm and full understanding of what it was that made all these what they are.

Make me aware of their broken hopes.

Touch me with a knowledge that in the long struggle of the years they, too, have found life hard.

Show me the fathers and mothers who dreamed of good things for their children that fate has denied.

Teach me, O God, this lesson in the school of life, to hate the evil things men do and to understand the forces that made them do these things.

And let me dare, some day, if now it is too costly, to

understand these forces so well that I can pray with One who suffered long ago, "Father, forgive them, for they know not what they do." In his name, Amen.[1]

MAKE ME A TRUE FRIEND

For the men and women of all ages who are my friends, I bring thee, O Lord, my humble and hearty thanks. For their unselfish loyalty and their steady faith I am glad and grateful.

Enable me to be true to them.

Grant me the courage to defend them when they are ridiculed or defamed.

Let me understand and rejoice in their virtues and be honestly aware of their faults.

May I be frank and kindly when I know them to be wrong, genuine in my admiration when they are right.

Give me a wise willingness to see that they are fully and accurately understood by others.

Thus, my Lord, grant that my friends and I may enrich each other as we travel the road of life together.

O God, make me a true friend. In the name of Him who said, "Ye are my friends." Amen.[2]

PRAYER FOR GOOD LEADERS

O God, send us leaders who aren't too easy on us— who hold up before us things to do that are entirely too hard for us (but we *try*, anyway!) . . . who let us know in no uncertain terms that they expect nothing less than our best (and they always seem to expect more than *we* think is our best) . . . who show us what it is to be strong, and not to give in to little disappointments or pains and aches or failures (and by their own strength, we seem to have more ourselves). Send us, O God, leaders who are *good* for us! Amen.[3]

WHEN FACING SOMETHING HARD

O God, when we have something disagreeable to do, or have to follow through on something we'd rather get out of, *hold us to Thy way!*

We want to learn, not just the simple, easy lessons of life that are before our eyes, but the hard ones, too.

When we have to stand some physical pain, may we think first of Thy love and not the pain. Help us to smile, so as to make it easier for others to stand things.

Save us from being sissies and pampering ourselves about little things. Make us strong like mountain climbers, for we want always to move up a little higher than before. Help us look up and not down, out and not in, forward and not back. And may we then be ready to lend a hand to someone else. Amen.[4]

REMEMBERING THOSE WHO HAVE GONE BEFORE

Feeling the bond of fellowship with those who have passed into the invisible realm, yet whom we remember with affection, let us pray:

Almighty Father, You have the whole world in Your hand—not just the world that we see now with our eyes but the world of all those who have gone before us.

We thank You for the lives of courageous, faithful ones. We want to be better because of them.

And now, lead them by green pastures and still waters into still higher life and service. For Your love leads us on, even through the valley of the shadow of death into a larger life.

Join us in a Fellowship Circle of loving remembrance. Amen.[5]

THANKFULNESS FOR PARENTS AND OTHERS

O Father God, we thank You now for our fathers and mothers; and not only for our own, but for all everywhere who are taking care of children and young people—in orphanages and refugee camps and anywhere. We couldn't live if our needs had not been taken care of, when we were too small to do things for ourselves. For all the loving care and help which has been ours, we thank You.

May we be the kind of persons that would make them happy—and make You happy, O God. Amen.[6]

PRAYER FOR STRENGTH OF PURPOSE

O God, so often we start out in the morning meaning to be good. We want to be clean and joyous and helpful all day. Then something happens, and first thing we know, we've spoken an unkind word and made a shadow come across somebody's face. Or we've done something we're ashamed of. What makes us like that, God? We're sorry and ashamed.

Somehow we feel You understand; You know what's weak inside us—make us strong. Forgive us, and help us to be understanding and forgiving toward others that may hurt us. Help us learn to love, from the bigness of Your love. Amen.[7]

PRAYER IN THE SPIRIT OF ST. FRANCIS

This prayer is in the spirit of St. Francis, gay "troubadour" for God. It is said that he was prone to go down to the village, and to draw a crowd for his message, would begin to play an imaginary violin, singing lustily and joyously. He liked to call himself and his band of mendicant monks, "jongleurs" or "minstrels" for God.

O God, we are Thy children; make us Thy Master-singers, too.

Sweep with the touch of Thy love our heartstrings, and awaken all the harmonies that slumber there.

Into this Thy kindergarten of souls Thou dost call us,

To work and play, to love and worship:
Help us to look up, lift up, and be glad.
So may the world rejoice. Amen.[8]

13

Scripture

SCRIPTURE THAT HELPS US LIVE

Passages that help us worship:
- I Chronicles 16:9
- Habakkuk 2:20
- Psalms 24:1; 33:5; 40:5; 98:1*a*; 118:29, 122:1

Pictures from God's created world:
- Psalms 8 (midnight beauty); 19:1-7 (sunrise glory); 29 (thunderstorm); 104 (song of the earth)

Ways Gods speaks to us:
- Genesis 9:12-14 (a rainbow in the sky)
- Exodus 3:1-6 (Moses finds God in a desert bush)
- Isaiah 41:19-20 (the work of God's hand)
- Jeremiah 23:23-24 (God fills heaven and earth)
- I Kings 19:8-13 (Elijah hears God's voice in the desert)
- Luke 12:27-31 (lilies of the field show us how to live)
- Matthew 4:18-22 (Jesus finds friends by the lake)
- Psalms 19:1-6 (the heavens declare)

All life is holy:
- Exodus 21:1; 22:6 (an early conservation rule)

Job 40:21-22 (God's never-failing goodness)
Matthew 10:28-31 (man greater than sparrows); 13:31-32 (mustard seed)
Psalms 93 (God rules, even in a storm)

Deuteronomy 8:6-9
Numbers 6: 24-26
Psalms 1:1-3; 8:3, 4; 28:7; 29:3-9; 65:9-13; 96; 104:24; 106:12; 136:1, 4, 5, 7, 8, 9; 139:1-12, 14-18, 23, 24; 147 (This may be read by choral choir by arranging so that all voices speak together the basic affirmations—at the beginning, midway, and at the close; then alternate men's and women's voices on the sentences between); 157
Song of Solomon 2:11-13

A UNIVERSE OF LAW AND ORDER, YET LOVING CARE

The physical universe:
Genesis 1:3-25; 2:8, 15; 8:22
Job 36:26-33; 37:5; 14*b*-18
Proverbs 6:6-8
Psalms 19; 104:10-24; 110:97; 147:15-18; 148:5-8, 10
Mark 13:28
Matthew 7:24-27

Persons the highest of God's creation:
I Corinthians 2:5-9*a*
Genesis 2:15
Galatians 6:7-8
John 6:27-29; 13:24
Matthew 6:24-25; 22:37-40
Philippians 4:8
Romans 8:28; 13:10; 14:7*a*

From the Sermon on the Mount, finding clues for living: Matthew, 5:3-5 (forget self, don't be conceited); 5:7 (be kind, considerate); 5:9 (be a *maker,* not just a keeper, of peace); 5:16 (do good); 5:22 (hold anger); 5:23-24; (if you do quarrel, be reconciled, apologize); 5:27-28 (respect others); 5:39 (return good for evil); 5:40 (even when people wrong you, give to them); 5:41 (do more than is expected); 5:43-44 (love all); 6:1 (don't be a "show-off"); 6:12, 14-15 (forgive); 6:19 (don't be a selfish prig); 6:25 (don't be a worrier); 6:33 (put the kingdom of God first); 7:1 (don't judge others); 7:3 (don't be always criticizing); 7:5 (help others overcome faults); 7:9-11 (give generously); 7:12 (treat others as you would have them treat you); 7:16 (evaluate others by their actions).

14

Aids to Worship

GRACES

Father, Thy gifts are before our eyes. We would not reach our hands to partake, until we have first thanked Thee. May we now enjoy these gifts, and feel Thee in our enjoyment. Amen.

Great Giver of every good and perfect gift, give us just one more gift—the gift of thankful hearts! Amen.

As we reach forth to accept from Thy hand these good gifts of food and friendship, wilt Thou reach forth and accept the thanks of our hearts. Amen.

We hesitate, O Father, to eat . . . we feel so unworthy. Thy goodness is so vast, Thy love is so kind. Make us worthy now, O Father, that we may live splendidly for Thee. Amen.

May our lives, renewed with the strengthening food we are about to partake, be lived nobly and wholeheartedly for Thee. Amen.

Our Father, we thank Thee now before this meal. May our lives thank Thee all the time. Amen.

Thank You, Father, for all who helped to grow and prepare this food and bless them wherever they may be. May we do our part in turn to help and bless others. Amen.

OFFERINGS

O Thou Giver of all good gifts, may these tokens be as a sign that we give Thee our hearts. Amen.

Grant, O Lord, that in our giving we may find Thee, for then we shall be rich indeed. Amen.

Accept, O Lord, this offering that comes from our hands and hearts. With it, we offer Thee our thoughts and lives. Amen.

As we give now for Thy work in other places, we reach our thoughts through Thee in love to all those who will be using this money to do Thy work. Amen.

All things come of Thee, O Lord,
And of Thine own have we given Thee.

OPENING CALLS TO PRAYER AND WORSHIP

Leader: The LORD be with you.
Answer: And with thy spirit.
Leader: Let us pray.
(*All kneeling, or bowing reverently*)
O Lord, show thy mercy upon us.
Answer: And grant us Thy salvation.
Leader: O GOD, make clean our hearts within us.
Answer: And take not Thy Holy Spirit from us.
(Then may follow the Collect for the Day or suitable prayer)

Micah 6:6-8
Psalms 34:3; 43:3-4; 100:2, 4, 5

When preparing to thank God for His gifts in the natural world, and our responsibility to care for these resources:
Genesis 1, 2 (noting especially 1:28-30; 2:9a, 15)

Out under the stars some still night:
Amos 5:8
Isaiah 40:26
Psalms 8:1, 3-9; 19:1-6

On a rainy day:
Psalms 65: 9-13

When contemplating the kindnesses of God to all His children and preparing to give thanks for some special gifts (such as newly found flowers, or rock deposits or shells):
Psalms 107:1, 9, 15, 22

When meeting in early evening, as the first stars come out, or as a small candle is lit (or candles one by one):
Psalms 43: 3, 4

When going into a place of worship, such as a green cathedral or brush arbor or the worship-place at camp or home:
Psalms 122:1

When considering our part in God's plan, both to worship and to serve:
Psalms 100: 2, 5

When considering the marvels of creation, how all things in nature (including ourselves) have stages or seasons of growth and it is all worked out according to a Plan:

Mark 4:28
Matthew 6:28

When we are bowed down, discouraged, or suffering and need the healing power of God's love:
John 5:8
Psalms 130:1

When we have glimpsed some new goal we want to strive with our utmost to attain; or have dedicated ourselves to some new purpose:
Philippians 3:13, 14

When in the dark night we see no stars, feel lost and lone and far away, even from God:
Psalms 40:8

When facing something extremely difficult—to do or to endure:
Deuteronomy 23:27; 33:25
Philippians 4:13

When perplexed or bewildered:
Isaiah 26:3
Luke 8:48
Mark 10:52
Matthew 9:22

When needing to remind ourselves of what things should be put first in life:
Luke 10:27; 22:23, 31

When needing to pluck up courage:
Ezekiel 2:1

When we are especially sorry for our sins and weaknesses and wrongdoing:
Mark 2:5, 9

When we are setting out upon some new task or mission:
II Corinthians 12:9
John 4:24
Psalms 1:3; 119: 97-104, 105

Leader: O give thanks unto the Lord, for he is good.
Answer: For His Loving-kindness endureth forever.
Leader: O that men would praise the Lord for His goodness, and for His wonderful works to the children of men.
Answer: For He satisfieth the longing soul, and filleth the hungry soul with goodness.
Leader: O Lord, open Thou our lips;
Answer: And our mouth shall show forth Thy praise.

Let all those that put their trust in Thee rejoice: let them ever shout for joy: let them also that love Thy name be joyful in Thee.

FOR WORLD BROTHERHOOD

Leader: One is your Father, who is in heaven; and all ye are brethren.
Answer: For God hath made of one blood all nations of men to dwell on all the face of the earth.
Leader: Therefore all things whatsoever ye would that men should do to you, do ye even so to them.
Answer: They shall beat their swords into plowshares, and their spears into pruning hooks: nation shall not lift up sword against nation, neither shall they learn war any more.

The Lord is in His holy temple; let all the earth keep silence before Him. (*Then let there be a brief silence in which each may prepare His heart for prayer and praise.*)

BENEDICTIONS

And now may the peace of God, which passes understanding, that peace which the world can neither give nor take away, be in our hearts, and abide with us forever. Amen.

O God, let the love of Thine which we have felt here together go now with us to our places of abode. Stir each heart with meaningful memories, and with a light of high purpose to live always for Thee. Amen.

Grant us Thy peace, O Father, upon our way now. Let the glow from the campfire and the eternal stars light an inner glow in each heart. Amen.

Be Thou our vision, O Lord. Our eyes tend just to see what's about us. Give us eyes of the soul to understand one another more clearly, and to see the divine in everyone with eyes akin to Thine. Lead us in the path we should go. Amen.

O Heart that beats with every human heart,
O Love that bleeds with every human tear—
help us now to know as never before how loving Thou art, and to go forth to be in turn more loving to all Thy children everywhere. May we help heal the hurts and bring Thy joy. Amen.

Now unto the King Eternal, Immortal, Invisible, the only Wise God, be honor and glory forever. Amen.

O God, remind us often of what we have learned and felt here—that we may not forget, but live more strongly and earnestly for Thee. Amen.

Unto Thee, the Lord of Love, be glory and praise forever. Amen.

Father, it has been good to be here. Grant that we may remember that Thou art everywhere. Go with us now into all the paths of our lives. Amen.

O Father, deliver us from weakness and sin. Make us strong and full of courage. Let Thy peace fill our hearts, now and forevermore. Amen.

Teach us that it is better to give than to receive; to forget ourselves than to put ourselves forward; to minister than to be ministered unto. In the name of Him Who came to show us what love is like. Amen.

Now unto Him that is able to keep us from falling, and to present us faultless before the presence of his glory with exceeding joy, To the only wise God our Saviour, be glory and majesty, dominion and power, both now and ever. Amen.

The LORD bless us and keep us;
The LORD make his face to shine upon us, and be gracious unto us;
The LORD lift up his countenance upon us, and give us peace. Amen.

Psalms 19:14
Our Father, we pray now for courage to carry out the dreams that are in our hearts. Amen.

May the silence of the hills,
The joy of the winds,
The peace of the fields,
The music of the birds,
The fire of the sun,
The strength of the trees,
And the faith of youth
In all of which is God
Be in your hearts.[1]

15

The Camping Experience

WHAT IS CAMP?

We might say that camp is a "place." We would covet for every camper green woods, lakes, bird calls, quiet sunsets—that his young heart may be warmly aware of a Creator Who has made "all things beautiful in their time." *But camp is more than a place.*

We might say that camp is a "plan." We would covet for every camper a program thoroughly alive at every step—not too crowded for comfort, yet abounding in opportunities for zestful adventuring all through each day. *Yet camp is more than a plan.*

Camp is what happens inside the campers—what they take home with them in their memories, in their new purposes, in their improved or newly acquired skills, in their friendships, in their appreciations, in their at-homeness with themselves and their physical universe and all others, in their awareness of a Power beyond themselves and of His way for the world. That's what camp is.[1]

I AM CAMP

I am camp.
I am sunlight, a sheen on the water, a mist on the mountains and stars.
I am a doorway out of the commonplace into a new adventuring experience.
I am a place where youth learns the joy of play without a sting, of fellowship without regrets, of creative effort that wearies not, of a good time that leaves no headache—or heartache—behind.
I am a new purpose for life that will make the years different.
I am Noise—and silence with a thrill in it.
I am Laughter—and resolution that seeks the comfort of the hills.
I am Energy—and the touch of loving service.
I am Youth—and the slowly emerging habits that make matured experience worthy.
I am Today—and also the Tomorrow that is being shaped.
I am a Giver of Gifts—that pass not away, that time will not deceive. I am Habits, Ideals, Ways of Livings, Confirmed Attitudes in the Soul of Youth.
Because I am all these, and more—I invite youth into fellowship with me.
I am Camp.[2]

GLORIA AT THE LAKESIDE

Clear! Clear!
Clear at the lakeside, O God,
Vision of thee!
Thee in the gull's soaring,
Thee in the sun's deepening,

Thee in the surf-song,
Thee in a thousand lovely hearts,
Young and lifted up;
Thee in the prayers rising like flame and fragrance
To the sky at evening;
Thee in our sleeping!

High, with the gray rock pinnacles and the spray,
My being cries:
"GLORIA IN EXCELSIS DEO!" [3]

GENEVA

This is the camp of my dreams.
The camp of the hilltop rendezvous with God.
The camp of worship that challenges and inspires.
The camp where play recreates the spirit and strengthens the body.
The camp of earnest study, disregarding prejudice and convention in the search for truth.
The camp where work is filled with a purpose and direction;
The camp that is not a place but a fellowship of joyous questing youth.
The camp that sees not color or position,
The camp that remembers One who walked on other hills beside another lake and taught men how to live.
This is the camp of my dreams. Geneva.[4]

PARAPHRASE OF PSALM 100

Do a goodly deed for the Lord, all ye faithful,
Serve the Lord with eagerness. Look for him in labor's daily chores.
Forget not that He is Almighty.

He gives us hands, lets us use those hands;
He gives us minds and souls sensitive to good.
Search the hills in modern business and try to heal.
Do not give up though tasks seem hopeless,
For He will help you.
Give Him a chance and his kingdom will be strong.[5]

DEAR CAMP DIRECTOR

(*Written by a father to the Camp Director on his son's going to camp, the boy's first time away from home*)

He means so very much to us,
This boy of ours you borrow.
He's the only one we've got,
Sole gift to the Tomorrow.

We gladly loan him to you,
For we know at Camp he'll grow.
You'll find him ever eager,
There's much he wants to know.

We know you'll treat him kindly,
As he explores the hills;
And fills his heart with wonder,
And fills his day with thrills.

But most of all, we pray you,
Please do not think us odd—
We hope at Camp he'll practice
Close fellowship with God.[6]

I THANK THEE FOR ADVENTURE

I thank Thee for Adventure, God,
And for a burning restlessness inside of me

That answers to the call of new bold ways
Of living more abundantly.

I thank Thee, God, for stalwart peaks that lift
Their hemlock fingers far into the blue;
For ancient trails that wind up rocky mountain sides,
To lead me up to purer air . . . and solitude . . . and Thee;
For streams that sing their merry way among the hills;
For winds that hum in trees at night,
And birds that answer one another's call
Before the bugler wakes to blow his reveille;

. . . . . .

For fellowship with those who also climb Adventure's trail,
And press with purpose high along ascending ways
Who, singing though the path be sometimes steep,
Make my way easier for me;

. . . . . .

These things, dear God, have brought me high Adventure.
Help me to keep them deep within my heart
As treasures rare—a precious gift from Thy great hand;
But not as keepsakes that have long outlived their use—
No, let them be to me a living, driving power to send me on
With trust and confidence in Thee, who made them all,
To new Adventure—steeper trails, and more of Him,
Whose spirit I have found beside the Lake. Amen.[7]

WHAT IS WORSHIP?

The Psalms are a beautiful expression of man's deepest feelings, his joy and anguish, wonder and devotion. Read some of the following: Psalms 8:23; 16:5-10; 19:1-6; 46:1-3; 65:9-13; 104; 90:1, 2; 148:1-13.

A group of boys and girls your age read Psalms 8 together. They discussed it, and this led their thinking to the things they had observed and learned at camp together. The next morning they incorporated their thoughts into the following psalm:

When we think of the wonderful things in the world:
How the ants make their homes and care for the young, and co-operate upon attack,
The rocks and how the lichen and moss grow upon them,
The saplings and how they bend over to obtain light,
The small birds that have the beautiful colors and sing the beautiful songs,
The bright red mushrooms coming out of the dark ground,
The fire and how it burns,
The way in which a tree rots away and helps to form soil,
The rocks which have their way of helping to refurnish the earth with good rich ground,
The way new trees grow out of dead stumps,
The plants which grow in hidden places,
The sun to shine by day and the moon and the stars to direct us by night.
Who are we that you are so thoughtful of us and talk with us in so many ways?
We stop to praise you for all these wonderful gifts.
As we praise, we wonder who we are and why we were placed in this beautiful world.

THINKING ABOUT WHAT WORSHIP MEANS

As this small group sat around a campfire and thought of what they had done together and had seen, do you think they felt close to God? Do you think that the next day and days after they would be more observing and thoughtful, more appreciative of the things about them? Is this sharing of life experiences, this sharing in appreciation, worship?

What is worship? What takes place when one worships? Is it necessary to have a planned program as in the church? Can it also be a spontaneous experience, lasting perhaps for just a moment, but causing one to feel very near to God? As you find a tiny violet, and think, "Isn't it beautiful? God has made so many beautiful things in this world." Could that be worship?

Is worship something that is experienced and felt deeply—something in which each individual must take part?

As you have a new awareness of the marvelous way in which God has made each of us dependent on the other, or are conscious for the first time of the dependability of God's laws, are you apt to worship God?

What is worship? Is it becoming better acquainted with God, feeling closer to him so that you rejoice in his love—or praying earnestly for help in those things that give you trouble—or being really sorry and asking forgiveness for your mistakes? Is it finding that you have new strength to think and act more as a Christian should?[8]

LITANY OF PRAISE AND DEDICATION

For the stillness of the forest,
We praise Thee, our Father.
For the valuable experiences in camping out,
We thank Thee, our Father.
For the beauty in the sky and the color of it,
We thank Thee, our Father.

For the songs of crickets, the summer tanager, frogs, whippoorwill, and owl,
We thank Thee, our Father.
For the good vespers at the swimming lake, the big rock, and the vesper glen,
We thank Thee, our Father.
For the good food we had at our own campfire and in the dining room,
We thank Thee, our Father.
For our fun in playing, working, and singing,
We thank Thee, our Father.
For man's wastefulness in cutting good wood and leaving it to rot,
We beg Thy forgiveness, our Father.
For the well-cultivated farms,
We thank Thee, our Father.
For our many new friends,
We thank Thee, our Father.
For our parents and our church who made it possible for us to come to this camp,
We thank Thee, our Father.
On the stones we brought to help with the building of a new dining hall,
We ask Thy blessing, our Father.
For the opportunity the Climbers had of placing stakes by the little pines to protect them,
We are thankful, our Father.
For the Trailblazers' joy in service through rebuilding the bridge to the vesper glen,
We are thankful, our Father.
For the pleasure the Wenepohs had in building a shelter for firewood for future campers,
We give Thee thanks, our Father.

Because we are Thy children and we have been given all
this beauty for our use, help us to use these gifts well,
We pray Thee, our Father. Amen.[9]

NEW PURPOSES FROM CAMP

I have been making discoveries about God as we find Him in the out-of-doors, in the Bible, in people, and especially in His Son, Jesus. I wish to follow his plan, for my life, and so I want to:

Begin each day thanking Him for keeping me through the night and giving a new day to me.

Attend Sunday School regularly.

Tell my friends who do not attend church about Jesus and try to get them to go to church and church school with me.

Attend my pastor's class of instruction when I am old enough so that I may learn what it means to be a Christian.

Contribute money regularly to my church's program to carry the "good news" of Jesus around the world.

To watch my language so that anyone may listen to me anytime and not be embarrassed.

To watch my tongue and temper on all occasions.

To be a good sport by doing my part of the work at home, or at school, or in my play wherever I am.

Daily try to "do unto others as I would that they should do unto me."

Make Jesus my "Friend" to help me wherever I am and in whatever I am doing.[10]

THESE HAVE I LOVED

At Kiamesha these have I known and loved:
The breathless wonder of a dawn-lit sky;

A fresh wind blowing, white clouds drifting by;
The emerald green of grasses wet with dew;
Red-gold of sunset, and the radiant hue
Of rainbows after silver-slanting showers;
The shy, faint fragrance of many-colored flowers;
An acrid smell of woodsmoke, slowly rising
From embers in the dark; the appetizing
Odor of good things cooking; laughter, song;
The boom of cannon as it rolls along
The distant hill; the vibrant clang of bell;
And low, clear bugle calls; and all the well-
Remembered voices; friendly clasp of hands;
And distant views; a rugged hill that stands
Always the same, yet changing with the moods
Of mist and rain; the solitude of woods
Washed white with moonlight—or a vision far
Across the hilltops to a flashing star;
The warm caress of blankets; and the deep
Strange sounds of night; the healing touch of sleep;
These have I loved, and O, a thousand more
Will throng upon my memory before
This last brief night shall end, as with the dawn
We part, these, too, shall vanish and be gone.
So summer ends and we have had our day;
Now sounds are hushed too soon and, far away
I pray, dear God above, may these remain;
O faithless loves, keep faith with me again.[11]

TO THE HILLS AGAIN

O to be out in the hills away,
Under a wide and wind-swept sky;
Something there is that seems to say:
Things that are lovely never die.

O to breathe deep of the scent of dawn,
Drifting through wet woods, blossom-hung;
Over the hill where the night has gone,
Bird throats swelling with songs unsung.

Loveliness lies on the hills at noon,
Sunlight is dancing down the breeze,
Moved by the lilt of a merry tune,
Played by the wind in the hemlock trees.

Never another moon may rise
Over my hills, but it shall bless
Each understanding heart that lies
Under the power of their peacefulness.[12]

LAST WILL AND TESTAMENT OF THE FOREST RUNNERS TO THE CAMPERS WHO FOLLOW US

We found this campsite in order, and we leave it in good order for you to use. Please use it with care, especially the firewood, so that you may enjoy it in the right way. We hope you will use the paths in order to save the beauties of nature around here—the little trees and the plants.

We will you these things:

The joy of the opening campfire service.

The way we got to know a small group of people real well.

Free night and its informal fun.

The sleep-out in the woods when God took care of us. (We hope you will take more time to remove the rocks and sticks and pile up leaves for a woods mattress.)

Enjoyment of the chef's good food, the cook-outs, the progressive dinner with some of the other groups, and the ice cream freezes. May you enjoy turning it and eating it!

Two baby birds found by a Forest Runner, and the current crop of bugs, ants, and chiggers—who by this time have millions of little ones. The hike to Farmer Brown's place, 205 degrees from the big rock. Look at the wasted trees on the way.

Vespers on the big rock, at the new lake, and in the vesper dell.

We hope you will like the idea that we are "tenants of God" and will use these things to the best use you know.[13]

THE AFTERGLOW

A day is done—
In golden splendor sinks the sun
Beyond horizon in the distant west;
But radiance lingers on—
The sky is overcast with shadows
That reflect the sun
As beaming rays illuminate the clouds
And they are bathed in radiant splendor—
Crimson, purple, orange, gold,
And deeper shadings
Far beyond descriptive powers of mind—
This radiance is not the sunset—
'Tis the afterglow.

Dear God, as I go home from camp,
Give me the afterglow.
May radiance of high moments linger on—
The greeting of the dawn with Thee,
The woodland warblings of a feathered choir,
The timid rabbit hopping into brush,

The rippling waters, and the cooling breeze;
The great, high moments with Thy presence real,
When spirit of the living God
Touched quickeningly mine own,
And challenges were new
And dedications real.
Give me a lingering sense of friendship
From the friendships made in camp,
Give me remembrance of the things I learned—
The skills of hand and mind—
Creative values which can ever live.
Dear God, I'm leaving camp,
Give me my afterglow.[14]

Sources

CHAPTER 1

1. Author and source unknown.

CHAPTER 2

1. Clarice M. Bowman, *Spiritual Values in Camping* (New York: Association Press, 1954).

CHAPTER 3

1. Author and source unknown.
2. Samuel Taylor Coleridge, from "The Rime of the Ancient Mariner."
3. Author and source unknown.

CHAPTER 4

1. Elizabeth Cushing Taylor, in *The Mayflower* (Boston: Pilgrim Press). Used by permission of the author and of the Pilgrim Press.
2. Jeanette E. Perkins, *As Children Worship* (Boston: Pilgrim Press, 1936), p. 76.
3. E. McE. Shields, *As the Day Begins* (Richmond, Va.: John Knox Press, 1940), Frontispiece.

4. Old folk song, arranged by Franciscus Nagler, in Sophie L. Fahs, *Leading Children in Worship* (Boston: Beacon Press, 1944), p. 22.

5. Used by permission of the New Jersey Council of Religious Education, Henry Reed Bowen, Secretary.

6. Olive W. Burt, *God Gave Me Eyes* (New York: Samuel Gabriel Sons & Co.), entire.

7. Edith F. Welker and Aimee A. Barber, *Thoughts of God for Boys and Girls* (New York: Harper & Bros., 1945), p. 216. Used by permission of the Connecticut Council of Churches, Inc.

8. Ellen E. Fraser, in *International Journal of Religious Education,* February, 1944, p. 32.

9. Mary Alice Jones, ed., *My Own Book of Prayers* (Chicago: Rand McNally and Co., 1938), p. 20.

10. Shields, *op. cit.,* January 13.

11. *Ibid.,* April 28.

12. Raymond Tifft Fuller, *Nature Quests and Quizzes* (New York: John Day Co., 1948), p. 43.

13. Written by the children of the Primary Department, Trinity Episcopal Church School, Hartford, Conn. Used by permission of the rector.

14. Mrs. Lydia C. Edmonson, in *Christian Home,* November, 1953, p. 54. Used by permission of her daughter, Mrs. Don Barney.

15. Nancy Byrd Turner. Used by permission of the author.

16. Clarice M. Bowman.

17. *Ibid.*

18. *Ibid.*

19. *Ibid.*

20. *Ibid.*

21. *Ibid.*

22. Elizabeth B. Jones, *Roundabout Me* (Indianapolis: Warner Press, 1953).

CHAPTER 5

1. Annie Willis McCullough in F. W. Danielson and G. W. Conant, *Songs for Little People* (Boston: Pilgrim Press, 1933), p. 47.
2. From *Thoughts of God for Boys and Girls* (Hartford, Conn.: Connecticut Council of Churches, Inc., 1942), p. 18.
3. Jones, ed., *My Own Book of Prayers,* pp. 34-35.
4. *Ibid.,* p. 36.
5. Mabel Niedermeyer, *This Is God's World* (St. Louis: Bethany Press, 1946), pp. 11-13.

CHAPTER 6

1. Author and source unknown.
2. Clarice M. Bowman.
3. Nancy Byrd Turner. Used by permission of the author.
4. Perkins, *As Children Worship.* Used by permission of publisher and author. This poem is set to music as "The World One Neighborhood" in *Children's Worship in the Church School* (New York: Harper & Bros., 1940), and in several other hymnals.
5. Author unknown. Quoted from Lillian Richter Reynolds, *At Home in God's World,* Camp Leader's Guide (2d ed.; Richmond, Va.: Board of Education, Presbyterian Church in the United States, 1950), p. 23.
6. Prayer used at Temple Israel, Boston.
7. Author and source unknown.
8. Florence M. Taylor, *Neighbors at Peace* (New York: Abingdon Press, 1938), pp. 111-12.
9. Adapted from information in *Christian World Facts* (New York: Friendship Press, 1952), p. 15.
10. From *Thoughts of God for Boys and Girls* (Hartford, Conn.: Connecticut Council of Churches, Inc., 1943), p. 39.
11. Lula Doyle Baird, *Indian Children* (New York: Abingdon Press. Copyright 1938, Whitmore and Smith), pp. 35-36.
12. Lois Lenski, "Living with Others," in *Thoughts of God for*

Boys and Girls (Hartford, Conn.: Connecticut Council of Churches, Inc., 1952), p. 26. Copyright by, and used by permission of, the author.

13. *Ibid.*, p. 30.

14. *Ibid.*, p. 31.

15. *Ibid.*, p. 35.

16. Dr. Alva Myrdal, director at that time of the Department of Social Affairs, United Nations; release, December 2, 1949.

17. Lenski, *op. cit.*, p. 32.

18. Niedermeyer, *This Is God's World,* pp. 25-26.

CHAPTER 7

1. Clarice M. Bowman.

2. *Ibid.*

3. *Ibid.*

CHAPTER 9

1. Written by girls of Camp Unami, Pa., and Sentinel Baptist Camps, N.H. Used by permission of Myrtle F. Auch, director.

2. *Ibid.*

3. From *The Morning Watch,* for Evangelical and Reformed camp leaders (Philadelphia: Christian Education Press, 1942), p. 7.

4. Written by a third year high school boy; quoted in Gerritt Verkuyl, *Adolescent Worship* (Westwood, N.J.: Fleming H. Revell Co., 1929), p. 19.

5. Written at Unami and Sentinel camps.

6. Written by junior campers at Burton on Vashon Island, Puget Sound. Used by permission of Gordon D. Forbes, director.

7. *Ibid.*

8. Author and source unknown.

9. Reynolds, *At Home in God's World,* p. 23.

10. Mrs. Carl H. King and Marion Craig, Camp Tekoa, N. C. Used by permission of the authors.

11. Reprinted from *The Poems of Henry Van Dyke* (New York: copyright 1911 by Charles Scribner's Sons; 1939, by Tertius Van Dyke). Used by permission of the publisher.

12. Fred Cook, Jr. (when fourteen years old), Camp Kiamesha, N.J. Used by permission of Harold E. Wands, director.

13. Author and source unknown.

14. Ruth F. Bowman (when fourteen years old).

15. J. G. Howard, *Bethany Church School Guide,* August, 1938, p. 341.

16. Anne Richardson (when thirteen years old).

17. J. Lester Hankins, in *Christian Home,* April, 1954, p. 55. Used by permission of the author.

18. Written at Unami and Sentinel camps.

19. Author and source unknown.

20. Written by Rev. H. Glen Lanier for tree-planting ceremony, Camp Tekoa, N.C. Used by permission of the author.

21. Author and source unknown.

22. Bertha Stevens, *How Miracles Abound* (New York: John Day Co., Inc., 1941), p. 124 and *passim.*

23. Author unknown. Poem fastened to a tree in one of the parks in Seville, Spain. Quoted by Fahs, *Leading Children in Worship,* p. 23.

24. C. L. Seidenspinner, *Our Dwelling Place* (New York: Abingdon Press. Copyright 1941 by Whitmore and Stone), p. 46.

25. Lydel Sims, "When the Stars Come Out," *Epworth League Meeting for Intermediates* (Nashville, Tenn.: Methodist Church Editorial Division, Board of Education, Department of Youth Publications, 1940), Vol. IV, No. 2, Program 2, pp. 2-3.

26. Christian Richardt, tr. by S. D. Rodholm, in *World of Song* (Des Moines, Iowa: Danish American Young People's League, Grandview College, 1941), I, 18.

27. Michael Pupin, "A Heavenly Language," in *From Immigrant to Inventor* (New York: Charles Scribner's Sons).

28. Kate McPherson, in Orene McIlwain, *Worship God* (rev. ed.; Richmond, Va.: John Knox Press, 1954), p. 131.

29. Clarabel Williams, "Sharing Discoveries," in *The Pro-*

gram Builder (Richmond, Va.: Board of Education, Presbyterian Church in the United States, 1943), p. 26.

30. Abbie Farwell Brown, "Overtones," in *Song of Sixpence* (New York: Houghton Mifflin Co. Copyright 1914 by Abbie Farwell Brown; 1942, by Barton Corneau), p. 47.

31. Stevens, *op. cit.*, p. 19.

32. Ruth Schuchart, Camp Beechwood, N.Y., in *Camping Magazine,* January, 1954, editorial page. Used by permission of *Camping Magazine.*

33. Mae Sigler, *Trails for Worship* (camper's book for use with *Our Part in God's Plan*) (New York: Abingdon Press. Copyright, 1951, Pierce and Smith), 8th day, pp. 18-19.

34. Walter Lowdermilk, *Conquest of the Land through Seven Thousand Years,* Agriculture Information Bulletin No. 99 (Washington, D.C.: Soil Conservation Service, U.S. Department of Agriculture, 1942), p. 17.

CHAPTER 10

1. Written at Unami and Sentinel camps.
2. Author and source unknown.
3. Reynolds, *At Home in God's World,* p. 39.
4. Author and source unknown.
5. Author and source unknown.
6. Chinese folk poem, 2500 B.C.
7. Old Indian song, carved on Capitol, Lincoln, Nebr.
8. Author and source unknown.
9. T. R. Alexander, in mimeographed book of meditations for Pittsburgh YMCA and Camp Laurel Ridge, Pa. Used by permission.
10. *Ibid.*
11. *Ibid.*
12. Clarice M. Bowman.

CHAPTER 11

1. John and Ruth Ensign, *Stewards in God's World,* a guide for junior high camp leaders (Richmond, Va.: John Knox Press, 1953), p. 87.

2. Dr. Rosalie Carter, of Carter Crafts, Franklin, Tenn. Used by permission of the author.

3. Wilson Jenkins, Camp Ohiyesa, Mich., 1929, as quoted in H. S. Dimock, *Character Education in the Summer Camp* (New York: Association Press, 1931), II, 47.

4. Nelle Morton, *My Camp Book: Living Together as Christians* (Philadelphia: Christian Education Press, 1952), p. 7.

5. *Ibid.*, pp. 30-31.

6. Percy R. Hayward. Used by permission of the author.

7. Creative writing from Camp Innabah', Pa.

8. Nelle Morton, *Living Together as Christians* (Philadelphia: Christian Education Press, 1952), p. 33.

9. *Ibid.*, p. 65.

10. Abba Hillel Silver, in *Christian Home,* April, 1954, p. 64. Used by permission of Rabbi Silver and of The Temple, Cleveland.

11. Alexander, in meditations for Pittsburgh YMCA and Camp Laurel Ridge, Pa.

12. From *The Friendly Story Caravan,* collected by a committee of the Philadelphia Yearly Meeting of Friends, Anna Pettit Broomell, chairman (Philadelphia: J. B. Lippincott Co. Copyright, 1948, 1949, by Anna Pettit Broomell), pp. 193-96.

13. Written for the Church Peace Union and World's Alliance by a committee of Youthbuilders, an organization of junior high boys and girls, 1948. Used by permission of the Church Peace Union and the World's Alliance.

14. Author and source unknown.

CHAPTER 12

1. Percy R. Hayward, *Young People's Prayers* (New York: Association Press, 1945), p. 76.

2. *Ibid.*, p. 3.

3. Clarice M. Bowman.

4. *Ibid.*

5. *Ibid.*

6. *Ibid.*

7. *Ibid.*

8. *Ibid.*

CHAPTER 14

1. Author and source unknown.

CHAPTER 15

1. Clarice M. Bowman, adapted from statement written by her in introduction to 2009-B, "Special Resources" (Nashville, Tenn.: Methodist Board of Education, Youth Department). Used by permission of Joseph W. Bell.

2. Percy R. Hayward. Used by permission of the author.

3. Martha Hazzard Mayer. Used by permission of the author.

4. Creative writing by unknown campers at Lake Geneva, Williams Bay, Wis.

5. *Ibid.*

6. Walter MacPeek, in *Camping Magazine,* January, 1954, editorial page. Used by permission of *Camping Magazine* and of the author.

7. Harold Patrick, Camp Adventure, N.C. Used by permission of the author.

8. Lynn and Campbell Loughmiller, *Let's Go Camping,* camper's book (New York: Abingdon Press, 1953), pp. 28-29.

9. Ensign and Ensign, *Stewards in God's World,* p. 89.

10. Written at New Lenox Methodist Junior Camp, Ill., Rev James H. Odom, director.

11. Harold E. Wands.

12. *Ibid.*

13. Ensign and Ensign, *op. cit.,* p. 59.

14. Rev. J. Dewey Muir, East Bay Camp, Bloomington, Ill. By permission of the author.